The EMPEROR'S STARGATE

Cheung Kwong Yin   **Alexandra Harteam**

a lotuseed publication

ISBN 962-86020-4-7

Contact: Billion Land Enterprises Limited
          9/F Flat A 18 Wong Chuk Hang Road   Hong Kong
          Tel: (852) 2553 7241   Fax: (852) 2518 7216
          E-mail: billland@netvigator.com
          Website: www.iching-tarot.com

To all the people, known and unknown to us, who are striving to be the best they can be.

CONTENTS

Introduction

Millennia ago, scientific observers in many diverse civilizations painstakingly recorded patterns of individual behavior and character which have managed to survive until the present. Today, we call these recorded patterns by a more or less common name – astrology. Since the Renaissance, astrology has been vilified as chicanery and increasingly dismissed by the growing body of Western scientific thought for its failure to yield to that body's evermore sophisticated explanations of who we are and how our world works. Yet, with each new generation, brought up with a growing bounty of scientific breakthroughs and high-tech wizardry, astrology refuses to simply fade away. Why?

Astrology endures, I suppose, because it speaks to a unique quality of the human condition. That quality is intuition – the 'place' in each of us where intellect and sensory input unite. Ironically, two to three thousand years ago, astrology embodied the synthetic process we have now bisected and labelled under the separate headings of intuition and science. Lacking our awesome analytic tools, ancient scientists depended on time and more time with which to record and revise their observations to coincide with and explain the world around them – an ongoing process that then, and now, yields what each of us continuously throughout a lifetime of learning comes to call our 'reality'.

But, while science's immense power is its ever-expanding ability to analyze and account for behavior on an increasing nanometric scale, the equally immense power of intuition is to see the whole and to synthesize apparent contradictions such that the greater whole embraces a reality under which such apparent contradictions do not just disappear, they unite. Take a few minutes to examine the biographies of some of our greatest modern scientists and you will find how often they credit their scientific breakthrough to intuition. And, who knows, had Pythagorean and not Platonic thought prevailed, we might all now today understand ourselves and our reality in a very different way. Perhaps, next time around.

Deeply rooted in intuitive observation and thought, astrology has only contributed to its own degradation by attempting to justify its knowledge and its relevance in terms of modern day science and its 'discoveries' such as cosmic rays and inter-planetary gravitational and electromagnetic fields. While it is true that the most intellectual and articulate of ancient civilizations looked skyward, rather than into the earth or the oceans, in their search for symbols and meaning, it is a demeaning and ultimately pointless exercise for practitioners to apologize for astrology's ancient language and mystical origins in an attempt to overturn its characterization as superstition and, moreover, to then attempt validation in the language of modern-day science. For, like music which is neither justified nor appreciated by the ancient shape and names of its notes, astrology can not be judged by its arcane symbols and terms but rather by its user's accumulated experience.

So for a moment, put away two things. First, set aside the immense "scientific" bias with which we are all now deeply inured. Secondly, and equally, set aside modern superstitions about ancient symbols and superstitions that characterize our impressions of astrology. Instead, look closely only at the experience – the "notes" if you will – that make up the chords and the rhythms of the pages of music which is your life. Don't panic. Such request is by no means an appeal to reject science and is far, far from it. For in reality, this is an invitation to actually apply the principals of classic science to observing the patterns of your own life by using your greatest personal scientific power – your intuition. And, like the scientific process we all know and accept today, the more rigorous and the more honest that inquiry, the more revealing are the results. So then, just as 'hot and cold' and 'up and down' yield to the relativity of thermodynamics and astrophysics, so do concepts such as 'good-bad' and 'right-wrong' disappear inside the more enlightened understanding that comprises the spiritual journey of our unique self-realization and, our humanity.

Arthur E. Yama
Investment Advisor

ℐoreword

HISTORY

The various divination schools of Old China right down to the present day are many. These comprise of Palmistry, Physiognomy (the art of judging character from facial characteristics), I-Ching, Joss Sticks, Animal Signs and Birth Hour calculations which include the 4-Pillars and 8-Character Systems and Zi Wei Dou Shu (The Emperor's Stargate).

The oldest records of Stargate date back to the Soong Dynasty (960 A.D. – 1279 A.D.). Within Stargate, especially where intricate birth calculations are concerned, can be found traces in various degrees, of much of the above divination tools. Animal Signs, Birth Hours, the 4-Pillars and 8-Character Calculations have all evolved into divination systems in their own right. These systems are part of The Emperor's Stargate. They are not all of it.

Over the centuries, across the Yuan (1271 A.D. – 1368 A.D.), Ming (1368 A.D. – 1644 A.D.) and Qing (1644 A.D. – 1911 A.D.) dynasties, more and more records of Stargate came to be discovered and kept. However, because they span nearly a thousand years which were interspersed by civil wars, invasions and natural catastrophes, these records are far from complete. Where near-complete records were found, these seem to contradict one another. It is an impossible task to discern the true records from the fake, the right from the wrong.

It is a fact that many Chinese textbooks deal with Zi Wei Dou Shu. Each professes its version to be the closest to the original, many copying from each other.

Let us not be overly taken with the history of Stargate.

At its core, The Emperor's Stargate is an intricate calculation system that leads one to build an extremely accurate birth chart. Based on this chart, the whole life is laid out, explained and understood and thus we are guided to be the best we can be.

In this first volume, we deal with the 32 major stars that tell us about our Self, our life's work, our loves and family. In this capacity, depending on the position of the various stars, one is shown the highest and lowest points one can expect throughout life, secondly, within each major 10-year period and then within any year.

Where one needs to go into more detail about a particular event – the whys, wherefores, how, when, expected outcome and simple ways to coax or prevent a happening – will also be dealt with.

A word on the stars. It is a matter of being true to history and tradition that we refer to what we put in the 12 houses as "stars". Except for the Sun and Moon which are from our own galaxy, the origins of all the others have been lost; so too as to who or what gave us all that original information on these "stars". Being the product of calculations and charts, these could have been named pegs, pawns or pebbles. But "stars" they shall remain. Each star has been aptly named by their originator to reflect the characters and interpretations that come with each. In their interpretation, the authors have done their best to keep to the spirit of the original names. In its nucleus, each star's character is neutral – neither good nor bad; they just are. This is an important stance to take when making interpretations.

THE EMPEROR'S STARGATE – WHAT IS IT?

Anyone who knows his exact time of birth can successfully use the Stargate. It is *not* necessary that the local time of birth be converted back to China's time. This is where Stargate deviates from being purely mathematical and converge into the esoteric. GMT time differences have no bearing on Stargate's ancient charts and tables that are still being used to draw up every birth chart. Provided that the exact birth time is known, it does not matter whether you were born in the U.S.A. or China. Using the local birth time, one always comes up with the most astoundingly accurate reading of the past. The diviner can then find out highly detailed information on the future.

It is at this point that doubts begin to set in for the listener. Can any prediction really be so detailed? Or is the diviner merely channeling or thinks he is doing that but actually making it up as he goes along? It is a fact with the Emperor's Stargate that nothing is channeled or invented for the listener. All information given has been recorded and you will find this between the covers of this book. Combinations of facts depend on the combinations of stars, their grade, whether brilliant or in retrograde, "attachments", etc. etc.

The crucial point lies in the interpreter's skills in integrating star combinations and meanings. To address this point, we have given, in chapter 9, a reading in retrospect of a world-famous figure. Suffice for the Stargate practitioner to understand the essence of what the divination meanings are saying. Very often, the reader will find astounding accuracy – a physical happening that is detailed precisely. At other times, look for its divinatory meaning: the answers are always there. It is within the Stargate's capacity to warn or give the go-ahead signal, giving details in no unclear terms where the danger/opportunity lies. Use this system to its fullest. All of Stargate's basic information is contained between the covers of this book.

WHAT IT ISN'T

Another major controversy surrounding Stargate, because of its high accuracy, is the question whether it is an absolute life's chronicle. In no uncertain terms, let us lay this argument to rest: It is not. The reasoning is simple: An absolute life's chronicle would occur only if every person born at the exact year, month, date and 2-hour session, would have exactly the same experience(s) throughout life. Let us make an assumption of China. If in the year 2001, its birth rate was 10,000,000. Divide this number by 365 (days), then divide the answer by 12 (there are 12 2-hour sessions in a day), the answer would be 2,283 babies born every 2 hours. The fact that 2,000+ people use one and the same birth chart begs the question: Can these 2,000+ people all simultaneously get married, have children, change jobs, lose loved ones, and eventually die in the same year? In the 20+ years that I have studied Stargate, I have come across several cases of two people sharing the exact same chart. These people would have very similar backgrounds and life experiences but they are far from exact. In your course of study in Stargate, do not forget this: We, the people around us, all play a part in creating our own destinies and in turn, influence those around us.

We are not dictated by Stargate, the very thought of which would make life passive and irresponsible. We push its wheels. This instrument called Stargate shows us what we have created thus far and where we may be headed for in the future. We then continue our creation process. We, as intelligent, spiritual beings, are all an intricate part of the on-going clockwork called The Emperor's Stargate.

WE ARE GIVEN THE KEY

The key is in how to successfully integrate the stars in the 12 sectors. Their positions, interplay and combinations all offer a unique meaning. For example, in any given sector, there may be one to several stars. With just three stars in a sector, each having just two traits, one gets 8 possibilities (2 x 2 x 2). This again leads to the disproof that Stargate is an absolute chronicle of the life.

Consider this: The pilot of a plane flying from one destination to another picks up a hurricane on his radar screen. He could be headed for certain disaster if he continued on his preassigned course. A decision is made to change course. Modern technology has allowed to us view impending disaster and avert it. A lot of the mystery, controversy and awe can be taken out of Stargate if everyone viewed it as simply a tool very similar to a weather forecast.

The Authors

一、定十二宮位天干表

生年＼十二宮	戊癸	丁壬	丙辛	乙庚	甲己
寅	甲	壬	庚	戊	丙
卯	乙	癸	辛	己	丁
辰	丙	甲	壬	庚	戊
巳	丁	乙	癸	辛	己
午	戊	丙	甲	壬	庚
未	己	丁	乙	癸	辛
申	庚	戊	丙	甲	壬
酉	辛	己	丁	乙	癸
戌	壬	庚	戊	丙	甲
亥	癸	辛	己	丁	乙
子	甲	壬	庚	戊	丙
丑	乙	癸	辛	己	丁

二、起命宮及身宮表

生時	命／身	十二	十一	十	九	八	七	六	五	四	三	二	正
子	命	丑	子	亥	戌	酉	申	未	午	巳	辰	卯	寅
子	身	丑	子	亥	戌	酉	申	未	午	巳	辰	卯	寅
丑	命	子	亥	戌	酉	申	未	午	巳	辰	卯	寅	丑
丑	身	寅	丑	子	亥	戌	酉	申	未	午	巳	辰	卯
寅	命	亥	戌	酉	申	未	午	巳	辰	卯	寅	丑	子
寅	身	卯	寅	丑	子	亥	戌	酉	申	未	午	巳	辰
卯	命	戌	酉	申	未	午	巳	辰	卯	寅	丑	子	亥
卯	身	辰	卯	寅	丑	子	亥	戌	酉	申	未	午	巳
辰	命	酉	申	未	午	巳	辰	卯	寅	丑	子	亥	戌
辰	身	巳	辰	卯	寅	丑	子	亥	戌	酉	申	未	午
巳	命	申	未	午	巳	辰	卯	寅	丑	子	亥	戌	酉
巳	身	午	巳	辰	卯	寅	丑	子	亥	戌	酉	申	未
午	命	未	午	巳	辰	卯	寅	丑	子	亥	戌	酉	申
午	身	未	午	巳	辰	卯	寅	丑	子	亥	戌	酉	申
未	命	午	巳	辰	卯	寅	丑	子	亥	戌	酉	申	未
未	身	申	未	午	巳	辰	卯	寅	丑	子	亥	戌	酉
申	命	巳	辰	卯	寅	丑	子	亥	戌	酉	申	未	午
申	身	酉	申	未	午	巳	辰	卯	寅	丑	子	亥	戌
酉	命	辰	卯	寅	丑	子	亥	戌	酉	申	未	午	巳
酉	身	戌	酉	申	未	午	巳	辰	卯	寅	丑	子	亥
戌	命	卯	寅	丑	子	亥	戌	酉	申	未	午	巳	辰
戌	身	亥	戌	酉	申	未	午	巳	辰	卯	寅	丑	子
亥	命	寅	丑	子	亥	戌	酉	申	未	午	巳	辰	卯
亥	身	子	亥	戌	酉	申	未	午	巳	辰	卯	寅	丑

四、起大限表

五行局	陰陽男女	父母宮	福德宮	田宅宮	事業宮	交友宮	遷移宮	疾厄宮	財帛宮	子女宮	夫妻宮	兄弟姊妹宮	命宮
水二局	陰女 陽男	12-21	22-31	32-41	42-51	52-61	62-71	72-81	82-91	92-101	102-111	112-121	2-11
水二局	陰男 陽女	112-121	102-111	92-101	82-91	72-81	62-71	52-61	42-51	32-41	22-31	12-21	2-11
木三局	陰女 陽男	13-22	23-32	33-42	43-52	53-62	63-72	73-82	83-92	93-102	103-112	113-122	3-12
木三局	陰男 陽女	113-122	103-112	93-102	83-92	73-82	63-72	53-62	43-52	33-42	23-32	13-22	3-12
金四局	陰女 陽男	14-23	24-33	34-43	44-53	54-63	64-73	74-83	84-93	94-103	104-113	114-123	4-13
金四局	陰男 陽女	114-123	104-113	94-103	84-93	74-83	64-73	54-63	44-53	34-43	24-33	14-23	4-13
土五局	陰女 陽男	15-24	25-34	35-44	45-54	55-64	65-74	75-84	85-94	95-104	105-114	115-124	5-14
土五局	陰男 陽女	115-124	105-114	95-104	85-94	75-84	65-74	55-64	45-54	35-44	25-34	15-24	5-14
火六局	陰女 陽男	16-25	26-35	36-45	46-55	56-65	66-75	76-85	86-95	96-105	106-115	116-125	6-15
火六局	陰男 陽女	116-125	106-115	96-105	86-95	76-85	66-75	56-65	46-55	36-45	26-35	16-25	6-15

五、起紫微星表

火六局	土五局	金四局	木三局	水二局	生日
酉寅寅	午申戌	亥卯辰	辰辰申	丑午亥	1 11 21
午卯未	亥丑卯	辰辰酉	丑巳亥	寅未子	2 12 22
亥亥辰	辰午申	丑寅午	寅申申	寅未子	3 13 23
辰申巳	丑卯巳	寅未未	巳巳酉	卯申丑	4 14 24
丑丑丑	寅辰午	子辰巳	寅午子	卯申丑	5 15 25
寅午戌	未酉亥	巳巳戌	卯酉酉	辰酉寅	6 16 26
戌卯卯	子寅辰	寅卯未	午午戌	辰酉寅	7 17 27
未辰申	巳未酉	卯申申	卯未丑	巳戌卯	8 18 28
子子巳	寅辰午	丑巳午	辰戌戌	巳戌卯	9 19 29
巳酉午	卯巳未	午午亥	未未亥	午亥辰	10 20 30

1 Teach yourself the Emperor's Stargate

Stargate is a powerful tool of inner transformation that can help you access your personal potential, to understand others, and to interpret events in your life and the world at large. You don't have to be an expert in Stargate to make it work for you. In this chapter, we'll walk you through the basics of the various elements that make up the birth chart. The charts *(opposite)*, are passed down from ancient texts of Stargate and are instrumental in placing the stars into the various houses, when they become brilliant or otherwise.

No fewer than 10 and as many as 18 charts need to be consulted to manually draw up a Stargate birthchart. But here is where we leave off – thanks to computerization. With the CD that is provided with this book, you literally take seconds to put together charts on your life, 10-year cycles or any particular year. From hereon, all you need do is understand the elements in your charts.

Quick Start

*Running the Emperor's
Stargate CD software*

To run the Emperor's Stargate birth chart software in your computer, first insert the enclosed CD-ROM into your CD drive. Stargate should immediately appear on your screen. If it does not, double-click to open "My Computer" then double-click on your D-drive (your CD drive). The following chart will appear, prompting you to enter the name, date and time of birth, male or female, etc.

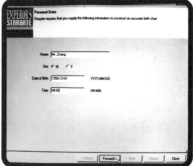

Click "Forward" and choose "Whole Life, "10-Year Period" or "Specific Years". Choose the specific year(s). Click "Forward".

If, for example, you have chosen a life analysis, a chart, similar to the one on the right will appear (with *all* details in *black*).

The 10-year chart (with relevant details pertaining to those years highlighted in *blue*) is shown below; and on the right – a specific year chart with details in *red*.

Life Chart (top right):

SPOUSE 2063-2072 106-115	PEERS 2073-2082 116-125	THE SELF 1963-1972 6-15	ELDERS 1973-1982 16-25
△ A1 Emperor ○ A13 General B22 Completion B25 Fire C29 The Lover	B17 Literary Minister B23 Ram C31 Opposition	B20 Delight B26 Bell B27 Void	B18 Arts Minister B21 Wing Horse
St4/Br6 Snake 9-11am	St5/Br7 Horse 11am-1pm	St6/Br8 Goat 1-3pm	St7/Br9 Monkey 3-5pm

MINORS 2053-2062 96-105	**THE EMPEROR'S STARGATE ON YOUR LIFE**		KARMIC 1983-1992 26-35
○ A2 Intelligence ■ ○ A12 Scholar B24 Spin Top	This Chart is for : Mr. Zhang You are a : Yang Male Chinese Birth Year : St5Br11 Chinese Birth Month : Lunar Month 10		× A6 Crimson △ A14 Pioneer
St3/Br5 Dragon 7-9am	Chinese Birth Date : 24th		St8/Br10 Rooster 5-7pm

PROSPERITY 2043-2052 86-95		PROPERTIES 1993-2002 36-45
○ A11 Mirror B28 Punishmt	You are born between : 7-9am Your animal sign is : The Dog	C32 Encounter

Color Code — Red - Year under review; Blue - The 10-Year Chart; Black - The Life Chart

The Catalysts — $ Prosperity; ○ Fame; ♫ Power; ■ Obstruction

Star Brightness — ● Brilliant; ○ Bright; △ Twinkling; × Dark

St2/Br4 Rabbit 5-7am			St9/Br11 Dog 7-9pm

HEALTH 2033-2042 76-85	TRAVEL 2023-2032 66-75	STAFF 2013-2022 56-65	CAREER 2003-2012 46-55
△ A3 Sun ♫ △ A10 Messenger	○ A4 Commander ■ △ A9 Opportunity $ B15 Left Minister B16 Right Minister B19 Stardust	△ A5 Waif ○ A8 Moon ○	● A7 Vault C30 Happiness
St1/Br3 Tiger 3-5am	St2/Br2 Ox 1-3am	St1/Br1 Rat 11pm-1am	St10/Br12 Pig 9-11pm

10-Year Chart (bottom left):

HEALTH · SPOUSE	PROSPERITY · PEERS	MINORS · THE SELF	SPOUSE · ELDERS
△ A1 Emperor ○ ○ A13 General B22 Completion B25 Fire C29 The Lover	B17 Literary Minister B23 Ram C31 Opposition	B20 Delight B26 Bell B27 Void	B18 Arts Minister B21 Wing Horse
St4/Br6 Snake 9-11am	St5/Br7 Horse 11am-1pm	St6/Br8 Goat 1-3pm	St7/Br9 Monkey 3-5pm

TRAVEL · MINORS	**Stargate for the 10-year period 36-45 (1993-2002)**		PEERS · KARMIC
● A2 Intelligence ■ ● A12 Scholar $ B24 Spin Top	This Chart is for : Mr. Zhang You are a : Yang Male Chinese Birth Year : St5Br11 Chinese Birth Month : Lunar Month 10		× A6 Crimson △ A14 Pioneer
St3/Br5 Dragon 7-9am	Chinese Birth Date : 24th		St8/Br10 Rooster 5-7pm

STAFF · PROSPERITY		THE SELF · PROPERTIES
○ A11 Mirror B28 Punishmt	You are born between : 7-9am Your animal sign is : The Dog	C32 Encounter

Color Code — Red - Year under review; Blue - The 10-Year Chart; Black - The Life Chart

The Catalysts — $ Prosperity; ○ Fame; ♫ Power; ■ Obstruction

Star Brightness — ● Brilliant; ○ Bright; △ Twinkling; × Dark

St2/Br4 Rabbit 5-7am			St9/Br11 Dog 7-9pm

CAREER · HEALTH	PROPERTIES · TRAVEL	KARMIC · STAFF	ELDERS · CAREER
△ A3 Sun ♫ △ A10 Messenger	○ A4 Commander ■ △ A9 Opportunity $ B15 Left Minister B16 Right Minister B19 Stardust	△ A5 Waif ○ A8 Moon ○	● A7 Vault ♫ C30 Happiness
St1/Br3 Tiger 3-5am	St2/Br2 Ox 1-3am	St1/Br1 Rat 11pm-1am	St10/Br12 Pig 9-11pm

Specific Year Chart (bottom right):

TRAVEL · HEALTH · SPOUSE	HEALTH · PROSPERITY · PEERS	PROSPERITY · MINORS · THE SELF	MINORS · SPOUSE · ELDERS
△ A1 Emperor ○♫ ○ A13 General B22 Completion B25 Fire C29 The Lover	B17 Literary Minister B23 Ram C31 Opposition	B20 Delight B26 Bell B27 Void	B18 Arts Minister B21 Wing Horse
St4/Br6 Snake 9-11am	St5/Br7 Horse 11am-1pm	St6/Br8 Goat 1-3pm	St7/Br9 Monkey 3-5pm

STAFF · TRAVEL · MINORS	**THE EMPEROR'S STARGATE FOR AGE 38 (1995)**		SPOUSE · PEERS · KARMIC
● A2 Intelligence ■ $ ● A12 Scholar $○ B24 Spin Top	This Chart is for : Mr. Zhang You are a : Yang Male Chinese Birth Year : St5Br11 Chinese Birth Month : Lunar Month 10		× A6 Crimson △ A14 Pioneer
St3/Br5 Dragon 7-9am	Chinese Birth Date : 24th		St8/Br10 Rooster 5-7pm

CAREER · STAFF · PROSPERITY		PEERS · THE SELF · PROPERTIES
○ A11 Mirror B28 Punishmt	You are born between : 7-9am Your animal sign is : The Dog	C32 Encounter

Color Code — Red - Year under review; Blue - The 10-Year Chart; Black - The Life Chart

The Catalysts — $ Prosperity; ○ Fame; ♫ Power; ■ Obstruction

Star Brightness — ● Brilliant; ○ Bright; △ Twinkling; × Dark

St2/Br4 Rabbit 5-7am			St9/Br11 Dog 7-9pm

PROPERTIES · CAREER · HEALTH	PROPERTIES · TRAVEL	ELDERS · KARMIC · STAFF	THE SELF · ELDERS · CAREER
△ A3 Sun ♫ △ A10 Messenger	○ A4 Commander ■ △ A9 Opportunity B15 Left Minister B16 Right Minister B19 Stardust	△ A5 Waif ○ A8 Moon ○	● A7 Vault ♫ C30 Happiness
St1/Br3 Tiger 3-5am	St2/Br2 Ox 1-3am	St1/Br1 Rat 11pm-1am	St10/Br12 Pig 9-11pm

Snake 9-11am	Horse 11am-1pm	Goat 1-3pm	Monkey 3-5pm
Dragon 7-9am			Rooster 5-7pm
Rabbit 5-7am			Dog 7-9pm
Tiger 3-5am	Ox 1-3am	Rat 11pm-1am	Pig 9-11pm

The Birth Chart

The Base Layer

We come to the concept of houses as we set up a specific birth chart, which is a map of the heavens at a given moment in time. Picture the Stargate chart as a mansion in the sky with a courtyard in the middle, and twelve dwellings all around it. This base layer is formed by the 12 Earthly Branches. These are the invariables. This level of the chart remains stationary and is the basis upon which every single individual chart is built.

For the sake of representation, we shall call these Earthly Branches by their Animal representations. You are probably familiar with your Chinese Animal Sign. Therefore, say, in a year of the Dragon, you will find the Self in the House of the Dragon. These earthly branches are also time sensitive. They pertain to the hours of the day. This layer is your calendar.

Branch 1: Rat : 11pm-1am
Branch 2 : Ox : 1-3am
Branch 3 : Tiger : 3-5am
Branch 4 : Rabbit : 5-7am
Branch 5 : Dragon : 7-9am
Branch 6 : Snake : 9-11am
Branch 7 : Horse : 11am-1pm
Branch 8 : Goat : 1pm-3pm
Branch 9 : Monkey : 3pm-5pm
Branch 10 : Rooster : 5pm-7pm
Branch 11 : Dog : 7pm-9pm
Branch 12 : Pig : 9pm-11pm

The first layer - The animals

Snake	Horse	Goat	Monkey
Dragon			Rooster
Rabbit			Dog
Tiger	Ox	Rat	Pig

The second layer - The Houses

PEERS	THE SELF	ELDERS	KARMIC
THE SPOUSE			PROPERTIES
MINORS			CAREER
PROSPERITY	HEALTH	TRAVEL	STAFF

Stars at opposite houses

Stars at 120°

The Second Layer

Superimpose the second layer, The Houses, which are the twelve areas of the life. A house is literally a 30-degree portion of the entire universe, viewed from where we are at the time of birth. The Houses represent the people and things that you hold dear . *Rotating clockwise* with each passing year, the Self, the people and things around us take on the characteristics of the stars sprinkled onto our chart at the precise time of birth. Following the Self are: Elders, Karmic Wealth, Properties, Career, Staff, Travel, Health, Prosperity, Minors, the Spouse, and Peers. This layer, like clockwork, moves one slot to the right every year. Therefore, if the Self were in the House of the Snake at present, by next year, in the year of the Horse, the Self would be in that House.

The Third Layer

The Third Layer are The Stars, which is an unmoving level and will be explained fully in the next chapter.Things happen within a house, but the house does not do anything itself – that's the job of the stars. The placements and groupings of the various stars remain constant from birth. Only the degree of brightness and the catalysts change. And as we (the second layer) move through this layer with each passing year, the houses and the people and things within them, come into their sphere of influence.

Reading your chart

At this point, it is worthwhile to mention that the stars from the opposite house and those at 120° *(Count 4 houses before or after – please refer to the diagrams opposite)* also influence any particular house we are studying. You will see this being mentioned throughout the book. It should be noted that the influence of stars at 120° are weak, probably a quarter of their real strength.

The Self *Destiny*

This is who you are. Who you will become in your place of birth. This encompasses the whole spectrum of what makes up the person – character, personality, physical traits, your perspectives. From the presence of various stars, the components that make up the person will be shown and in turn these will tell the career and the spiritual path you are likely to follow. In general, your life's path is revealed here.

Elders *Parents, family home, Parental home? see P.148*

One's relationship with one's parents, mentors (teachers) or employers, superiors and, for business owners, the (governmental) officials who cross your path; also clients, if you are a business owner. In other words, this house deals with people you put above yourself.

The emotional and psychological make-up is closely tied with the parent issue. Did you get parental protection as a child? Was emotional support lavished or withheld? Did your parents provide you with the educational tools needed for your future success? Are you close to either or both parents?

Karmic Wealth *Luck?*

This house governs intellectual and mental health. Whether one has a quick and agile mind is deduced here. Also, an important house to consider when divining a person's perceived quality of life – more so than the Prosperity or Career Houses. This house governs our emotional well-being – in general, our ability to appreciate what we have. Is one contented and happy with life's lot or emotionally unstable and miserable in the midst of great wealth? This is the house that rules spiritual, not physical wealth.

Properties/Business

Assets *Real Estate*

One's home or living conditions, the properties that you own and ultimately the state of affairs in your company if you are a business owner. This house also deals with inheritance. On a day-to-day level, one can see the general environment in which one works and resides. Neighbors, and the relationship with these people are also revealed.

Contemplating starting your own business? The stars in this house will tell you how you will fare.

Career

Vocation, endeavors that require no investment of your own money into it — being employed or being an independent consultant falls in this house

see P.171

In one's life path, what career to follow that will give the most joy and abundance. What to avoid. Career-wise, the general atmosphere one is to expect is seen here. Comparing the stars in the Property and Career houses reveals whether one's successes lie in being a business-owner or a salary-earner. In fact, check out both for your earning capacity. Pay close attention to the Career house if you consider yourself a salary-earner.

Staff

Friends?

The people who support you – employees or those working under you. Note this distinction: To find out the quality and what is going on with, say, 200 people working for you, check this information out in this house. However, among this 200, there may be two or more deputies or chiefs of staff who represent you. These two then should be considered under the "Minors" House.

Travel/Relocation

Embarking on a path of new, unfamiliar and adventures endeavors?

Public Relations

Travel meant danger, unknown, and adventurous and risky tasks in the ancient times!

What happens to the person should she migrate to another country. A study of the different stars in this House will indicate whether migrating to a foreign land is suitable. Interactions with foreigners, happenings when in a foreign land, or both.

Health

One's general physical health at various points in the lifetime. Also, hidden illnesses one may be prone to, physical impairment or internal disorders.

Prosperity

Finances

This house deals with liquidity and profit. An interesting point here is it is written in the stars in no uncertain terms whether or not one is to acquire great wealth. As can be expected, most of us looking up this House will find we are destined to have 'ordinary prosperity' here! How, how long it takes, and in what ways, to accumulate your wealth are all set out.

Minors *Children*

Again, a specific relationship house which covers your children, students and senior employees. Here, we deal with the general health and closeness or otherwise of the relationship. This house also tell us about family pets.

The Spouse *Union*

The house that governs the major romantic attachments during one's lifetime. The stars in residence describes the people one is romantically involved with in each specific period of one's life. Specifics include whether a spouse is supportive or not, degrades or enhances one's quality of life, the length of a relationship, physical traits and age difference.

Peers *Brothers*

The last house whereby the number of siblings and quality of the relationship are discussed. This is also the house for working partners, friends, colleagues, fellow students – i.e. people on your own level. Also, what goes on with the competition. Here is where you find out about the strengths and weaknesses of your rivals.

2 *The Stars*

Let us assume they are from other galaxies and that through them we are bound to the entire universe …

Zi Wei Dou Shu, or The Emperor's Stargate, is a complex, mathematical grouping of over 114+ pointers or "stars". The various stars that occur in each of the 12 houses at the exact time of birth determines the quality of life that a person is very likely to lead – it is the blueprint of life, so to speak. Of these over 114 stars there are 14 'major' shiners which, at different times, fall into any of four brightness categories according to their positions at the time of birth or divination.

The 14 major stars are the subject of this book. Each of these possesses a number of core, fundamental qualities, which together, make up the backbone of the birth-chart.

The Stars and Their Positions

All the 114 stars of the Emperor's Stargate, each working with the qualities and influence of other stars, make up the birth chart of the person. Of these, there are 14 stars which are the highlight of this book. Each of these stars contain very complex traits, such that each one takes on a unique character. Their interplay with one another, especially in opposing sectors, make up the major events that a person can expect throughout life. The remaining 100 or so stars, being less complex, but nonetheless providing further insight, will be discussed in subsequent volumes.

Star Brightness

Brilliant ◉

A brilliant star gives forth its most positive qualities. It has the ability to avert the evil influences of the *obstruction catalyst* or dim the detrimental powers of the *dark stars*. In the presence of other brilliants, a strong and auspicious house will be created.

Bright ◯

An auspicious star at its best, possessing the strong, positive qualities of the major stars. However, strains of the negative are present, which will be enhanced with the *obstruction catalyst* in the same or opposite house. Depending on the influence of the *dark stars* in the same or opposing house, positive qualities may become weakened or nutralized.

Twinkling △

In its weak state, a twinkling star tries but only manages to deliver equal amounts of the good and evil qualities of the major stars. A twinkling star bends towards the negative and the *obstruction catalyst* or any of the *dark stars* will exert considerable influence and destruction. A twinkling major star will be rendered useless against these and, depending on their detrimental influence, may even turn dark.

Dark ✕

A major star in retrograde, whereby all of its weaknesses come to the fore, obliterating the positive traits. Nutralized at its best by surrounding positive bright stars, a dark major star will have the negative enhanced by the *obstruction catalyst* or any of the *dark stars*. Look for redeeming qualities in the surrounding stars. Otherwise, expect a darkened house – a time to lie low.

A1. The Emperor (紫微)

AUTHORITATIVE, PIONEERING, CONQUERING, FAR-SIGHTED, HOT TEMPERED

The most important star that gives the Emperor's Stargate its name. This star displays all the qualities of a strong, wise, courageous monarch – a natural, pioneering leader who looks at the big picture. This individual displays a fiery temper. At its zenith, it enriches and banishes evil. In fact, it is so strong that it accommodates more than eradicate. For example, the Intensifiers (e.g. The Ram, Spinning Top, Fire, Bell, The Void or Punishment: C23-C28) can all be eradicated, or altered, by the presence of The Emperor. A leader in every sense of the word, it evokes power and elegance and invokes respect.

However, this is not a stand-alone star. As an emperor needs his ministers and warlords, this star, alas, will not shine alone. In aid of The Emperor, preferably, are the presence of his Left and Right Ministers (B15 & B16). Further on, there should be his Literary Minister (B17) and his Arts Minister (B18). And to keep things light, let's call in Stardust (B19) and Delight (B20), the angelic beings. This makes up the perfect court – The Emperor surrounded by his entourage.

So, what happens when The Emperor is present in a birth chart without any of his aides in sight? The negative, detrimental qualities of this star will be turned on. Reminiscent of an exiled Emperor who sits alone on his throne in an empty court, this star, if alone, will turn on frustration, anger and tyranny. A lone Emperor suggests isolation and loneliness.

A2. Intelligence (天機)

STRATEGY, PIONEERING, MOVEMENTS (LATERAL), MECHANICS, AGILITY

A balanced, strong mind breeds a kind leader who is calm but motivated. This star brings in a quick, intelligent mind that is interested in a wide range of subjects spanning the arts and sciences. This person thirsts for knowledge and has a quick mind and agile body. Alas, intrigued by anything that is new and pioneering, he may spread himself too thin and become a Jack-of-all-Trades but master of none. Intelligence is a strategist by nature and is mechanically inclined. The presence of this star indicates lateral movements – a change of job or duties as opposed to moving up the corporate ladder.

Easily distracted, Intelligence may find his powers dimmed or have his negative qualities surfaced should he meet with such dark stars as The Void or Punishment. Under dark influences, fear, self-doubt and despair set in. This negative star combination bodes ill for an entrepreneur. At its best, Intelligence shines on steady employees, not entrepreneurs or business owners. As an employee, Intelligence can look to apply all his positive traits to good use and will rise to great heights.

A3. *The Sun* (太陽)

BENEVOLENCE, YANG, MASCULINITY, OPENNESS, STATUS, ELEGANCE

*E*legance would be the jewel on The Sun's gleaming golden crown; his position being second to none but the Emperor. The Sun stands for all that is fiery, cleansing and positive. At his brightest, none would fail to be appreciative and warmed by his benevolent, powerful rays. A brilliant Sun would just leave good fortune at his wake and wouldn't even notice he had done that – so, would not expect to be thanked. Independent, helpful and FUN! Who could help but love him! Even if he didn't reap vast fortunes – and very often he doesn't because he simply doesn't care for these – his name will be etched in stone; or at least in the hearts of many.

The Sun also stands for the Father and the fortunes of this parent can be deduced by The Sun's position and level of brightness in the birth chart. At the absence of this parent (death) this star stands for the male self. In the case of a woman, this star would represent her spouse (if alive), or her (first-born) son if The Sun falls in her Self house.

This star in the Self house of either male or female, with or without any supportive or dark stars, indicates a lukewarm relationship with the male parent during one's formative years.

Now, the best place for The Sun would be the Career sector – where all of its most positive qualities would be able to shine through. The brighter the star the better. So, should the Career sector fall into the House of the Horse (11am – 1pm) with the supreme Sun in position, this person will rise to great heights in her chosen field.

A Brilliant Sun would be able to transform the powers of any of the six dark stars (A23 - A28): The Ram, Spinning Top, Fire, Bell, The Void or Punishment. Under this circumstance, only the males around the Self would be affected. The self would encounter certain difficulties as presented by these dark stars. However, The Sun is a strong enough influence to block any serious damage.

This benevolent star displays its positive energies between the hours 11am to 3pm. From thence onwards, The Sun would be in darkness. A dark Sun would want recognition to any good work it cares to do – and more often than not, this should preferably come in the form of monetary gains. Elegance then takes a back seat. A dark Sun goes on to amass great wealth. A dark Sun has the qualities of a Brilliant Moon.

A4. The Commander (武曲)

WEALTH, MANAGEMENT, ENTREPRENEURIAL SKILLS, HANDICRAFTS, METALS

Star of Earnings and rewards P. 169

Commander in the Self sector people are often slightly built with a strong, clear voice. This is a major star of action having to do with wealth. There will be major prosperity problems should this star be obstructed. You will be chasing wealth but it will never be in your grasp. The Commander is a decisive leader who leads his army into battle. Strong and determined, this star will lead its owner to success if found in the Career sector. If aided by other positive stars, expect entrepreneurial success. You should definitely start your own business with this star in your Properties/Business sector! *(However, with the Obstruction Catalyst attached – give up any such hope!)*

Happiness see p. 141

Watch out for Power (C30) which enhances The Commander. This makes for an outstanding partnership which is conducive to a career in the Corps. Chiefs of units and military commanders will usually have this star combination in their chart.

Fiercely independent, the Commander makes for a menacing guest if found in the Spouse sector. This star indicates a strong-willed and forthright individual.

A5. The Waif (天同)

EMOTIONAL, ENJOYMENT, SENSITIVITY, GENTLENESS, BUILDING FROM NOTHING

Contented by nature, The Waif goes through life as a happy-go-lucky little girl. There isn't a streak of competitiveness in her. She's happy to let you shine. It can be aggravating if you're looking for advancement and find this star in your Career house. Her saving grace, though, is her very nature. Her presence counteracts evil and averts disaster! Yes, she IS a little lucky, twinkling star that silences Bell and cools Fire and sweeps out the what-nots of the other four darks sisters. As contrarian laws go, these dark stars does a world of good for The Waif. In their presence, this star eschews some of her slovenly ways and actually moves forward with creativity and aplomb!

The Waif does well if found in the house of Karmic Wealth. She has the ability to build from nothing; or, with the ignition of the (dormant) fire in her, she amasses great tenacity and could even regain fortunes lost.

However, if she happens to fall into the Self or Career houses and with the absence of the albeit dark stars to prod her on, this individual becomes too complacent, even slovenly. It is apparent this star does little for career advancement.

The Waif in the Self House brings in emotional volatility, and a hard childhood. The individual with The Waif in the Self will be fair-skinned, have a squarish-round face and round shoulders. She will be gracious – a learned, gentle soul leaning towards the arts. She will spend much time in idealistic contemplation and a contented dreamer she is likely to remain.

A6. *Crimson* (廉貞)

BLOOD RELATIONS, EMOTIONS, ARTS, POLITICS, PRIVACY, FEMININE

A flirtatious number with a twinkle in his eye! Depending on where this star comes to rest, the degrees of success for career advancement could be gauged. Cut out for social activities, the individual with Crimson in his Career sector will find himself basking in attention and, ultimately, success. This individual will soar above the rest whether he is in PR or politics. Just put him amongst the crowd. The girls love him!

The individual with Crimson in the Career sector will do famously well in situations which require constant communication/dealings with the opposite sex; e.g. a man in perfumery, cosmetics, or lingerie; a woman in finance, athletics or any sector of business traditionally dominated by men. Crimson can expect to shine if found in the Career sector. And if there are other auspicious stars around – this career can expect a lift-off!

Crimson in the Self sector makes for a splendidly munificent personality. This is not one to count the small change. Independent and cheerful, he takes life's ups and downs at his stride and views set-backs as lessons. If they don't like him, he'll just wipe the egg off his face and not before too long, he'll be back. Yes, this one has a good back-bone and, should he need it, support is all around.

A point to note, however, is this star could mean very different things depending on its position and the presence of other stars. Grouped with other auspicious stars, the individual could rise to great heights, especially in politics. Inauspicious stars around Crimson could spell disasters of the life-threatening kind, having to do with blood. In this situation, great care should be taken with interpretation.

A7. The Vault (天府)

PROSPERITY, POSSESSIONS, PRESERVATION, CAREFULNESS, INTEGRITY

A major prosperity star from the conservative faction. As The Emperor rules the North, so the Vault rules the South. As the Emperor pioneers, so the Vault guards. Safely trekking paths hewn and hacked by others before him, the Vault quietly builds her fortunes. This star would shine on careers having to do with administration and management. And who says these individuals, given tenacity and hard work, will not reach as high or higher than, her more daring sisters?

The Vault in the Self sector produces outstanding and high-ranking administrators and government officials. What they lack in pioneering savvy, they make up for in prudence, groundedness and caution. If free of any dark stars, these individuals become the pillars of the earth. They live by honesty and integrity.

18. The Moon (太陰)

NIGHT, FEMININE, TRANQUILITY, RETIRING, GRACEFUL, WEALTH

T he Moon is at her most brilliant during the hours 9pm to 3am. Outside of these, she is in darkness. It is a point to note that the hours of influence of a brilliant Moon is the direct opposite to that of The Sun. Because of this, whereas a brilliant Sun promotes grace and elegance – the spiritual qualities, The Moon adorns with the physical. Together, these make up the Chinese characters for Abundance (富貴).

The Moon also stands for female or the female parent. The fortunes of this parent can be deduced by The Moon's position and level of brightness in the birth chart. At the absence of this parent (death) The Moon stands for the female self. In the case of a man, this star would represent his spouse (if alive), or his (first-born) daughter if The Moon falls in his Self house.

The Moon – be it Brilliant or Dark, in the Self house of either male or female, with or without any supportive or dark stars, denotes a lukewarm relationship with the female parent during one's formative years. If in the male Self sector, this star indicates heightened, positive female qualities. For example, he may display gentle strength, be supportive and encouraging, intuitive and excel at or at least be very keen on what is traditionally labeled female domain e.g. cooking (although most of the world's best chefs are male!). This male self will also find empathy more with female than male colleagues and friends.

A woman with a brilliant Moon in the Self sector will be

beautiful, romantic, a home-maker and very supportive of her spouse and family. Whether male or female, The Moon in the Self sector makes for a strong, mature individual who is also clever and introspective. The Moon in darkness has the qualities of a Brilliant Sun.

19. Opportunity (貪狼)

INDULGENCE, SENSUOUSNESS, PHYSIQUE, MUSCLES, SPORTS, DIVINATION

Full of sensual magnetism, one seizes the opportunity and milks it for all its worth. He who possesses Opportunity in his Self House will be refined and conversant in the arts and well versed in the latest of what is in fashion. He relishes every bit the interest he creates and adores the attention he gets in the seemingly inexhaustive rounds of meetings and partying. An opportunist to the core, he has a different mask for each occasion and therefore has many superficial sets of 'friends' – from the highest echelons of society right down to the underworld. Because, in the end, everything has to do with power.

Opportunity in the Self sector, if coupled with one or more positive stars denote a long life. This person will also have other-worldly, spiritual leanings and he will find himself dabbling in astrology or other forms of divination. He also lavishes all the sensual pleasures he could gather on himself. The finest culinary fare, the arts, people who would pander to him – he's tried everything.

It is to be remembered that where Opportunity appears, its two other brothers, The General (A13) or The Pioneer (A14) are not far away. Any point in time where these three stars appear together is an indication for turbulence and great change.

A10. *The Messenger* (巨門)

SLANDER, LITIGATION, CAREFULNESS, PRIVACY, SUSPICION, LARGENESS

Messenger in the Self sector indicates outstanding rhetoric abilities. Coupled with sharp diplomatic skills that are associated with the star, this is surely an obvious prompt for any career path! Alas, much controversy surrounds such a prominent individual.

She who has The Messenger in her Self house will also always be on the go – and we're not talking about smooth sailing here. Not born with a silver spoon in her mouth, the struggle uphill will have begun early in life. Anticipate a long, albeit exciting road ahead.

An eloquent speaker, The Messenger is best suited to be in any career that entails selling, marketing, speaking for or promoting issues close to her heart. For here is where she excels and will find satisfaction. The Messenger shines in any career that makes her voice heard.

A11. The Mirror (天相)

Leverage? **REPEATING, HELPFULNESS, RESPONSIBILITY, INFLUENCE, EMBROILMENT**

Bearing the seal of the Emperor, The Mirror endorses every edict that is passed down. The outstanding feature for the Mirror is therefore Responsibility. Here, if ever, is a responsible individual – be it to himself or to those close to him. He sees himself as totally answerable to everything that he puts his seal on – a just and impartial individual. When and only when he is satisfied with the details will he carefully endorse with his seal. And no smudges please! This individual will be recognized by the care and detail he applies to his dress, home and office.

The Mirror in the Self indicates a careful individual. Where everyone else has already jumped in, he would still be busy plugging up the holes. Upright and blessed with a big heart, he just fits right into everyone's ideal of the big brother. Well, he doesn't at all mind helping out. In fact, if necessary, he will go out of his way to fight for what he believes in.

Blessed with great tenacity, the Mirror in the Career house points to one unswerving career (or employer) throughout the whole working life. And his responsibility and care will have huge dividend pay-offs. He will rise above the rest.

Heads of large organizations will not fail to benefit to have the loyal Mirror by their side. Ministers, secretaries – anyone who is second-in-command will have this star in his career chart.

The power of a Brilliant Mirror greatly outshines any of the dark stars. In its dark hours or surrounded by dark stars without the help of any positive ones, the Mirror's positive energy will diminish, making the individual self-protective and suspicious.

A12. The Scholar (天梁)

Not one to toil and struggle, The Scholar displays a certain degree of elegance as he pursues the good, easy life. This star in the Self sector indicates longevity, but alas a lonesome existence. The scholar will have a high opinion of himself. He has his own set of rules and cannot be easily swayed. In the presence of dark stars, Scholar turns into a self-righteous, vain individual.

The Scholar in itself is a lucky star, upholding principles and orderliness. Its presence in any sector ensures that major disasters or setbacks can be averted or at least diminished. Scholar deals with the elderly, medication, insurance, accountancy, numbers and the uniformed forces.

A friendly, auspicious star on the whole; but its brightness at best reaches only the Twinkling level. Not to be confused with the Brilliant benevolent powers of the Mirror (A11); and its elegance is but a glow compared to Sun's.

The presence of Scholar indicates a profession in teaching or administration. Possessing his own brand of pride, Scholar would be positively not suited to any entrepreneurial pursuits of his own. For business entails monetary transactions – and money goes against every grain of Scholar's opinion of what is lofty and right. In the presence of the dark stars, if in business, Scholar will get embroiled in some curious 'accidents' involving money. Money, or the lack of it, is Scholar's life lesson.

A13. The General (七殺)

SEVERITY, STRATEGY, INDEPENDENCE, ALOOFNESS, STAGNANT, HESITATION

One of the major stars which support the Emperor. Whereas The Pioneer (A14) is out there at the front-line, the General is the brain behind the scenes. The General is a cool-headed strategist – and one to be reckoned with. He commands respect and can hold court alone in any sector. If ever, here is one star that shines if left utterly alone.

Whether male or female, the General in the Self or Career sector is a sure indicator of a brilliant career. One of the General's outstanding traits is that he jealously guards his independence. When found in one of the relationship houses, for example The Elders, Spouse or Minors House, he will appear aloof and distant to those close to him and become a cause for disappointment and sadness.

This is a person with great tenacity, will set goals and overcome any obstacle in order to get there. Not unlike The Pioneer (A14), this individual will have his share of turbulence (to a slightly lesser degree) for both immediately respond to the beckoning of adventure, even danger.

This star in the Career sector will leave a mark of outstanding achievementments in core management in large, multi-national corporations.

A14. The Pioneer (破軍)

DISCARDING THE OLD FOR THE NEW, HOPE, PIONEERING, HOT TEMPERED

Supporting and protecting the Emperor, this star fighter is constantly in the thick of battle. He charges forward with total disregard of his own safety, fighting for and protecting his turf. The Pioneer, one of the tri-star formation (the other two being A9 Opportunity and A13 The General), stands for great changes, uprooting and tearing down. Fasten your seatbelts, please.

The year that The Pioneer appears will be a time for the greatest upheavals, with life-shattering consequences – not a pleasant experience for the faint-hearted. At this point, it is well to remember that change is only change. It forces your car down another, albeit unexpected road. And don't forget, Opportunity (A9) or The General (A13) will always be there to meet you. Take the reigns and embark on this exciting journey!

Yes, many will find fault with The Pioneer. He is headstrong and overbearing, they say. But we suspect they all secretly admire this tenacious one who charges on regardless. They see the pioneering spirit and his brave heart and didn't they follow and was benefited by his leadership?

Quick to anger, The Pioneer benefits with having the Emperor (A1) around – the highest authority and the only one who could subdue him. The Emperor lessens the throes of upheaval caused by The Pioneer and ensures a smooth transition.

Whether male or female, The Pioneer in the Career sector indicates inventiveness and success. Let this fantastic energy flow towards the building of new ideas and challenges. This will be a hard-working professional or craftsman in the highest order. You will not find him snoozing in your armchair.

The Stars in Each House

The meaning of each star as it falls
into each sector …

The 14 majors stars, as they take up residence in the different sectors of the Birth Chart, assume different meanings for The Self. These are their characteristics or divination meanings:

Note: Stars in opposite house or houses at 120° influence a house, but these influences (see Chapters 9 & 10 for examples) seem to different from the influence of the same stars in the house under consideration. But, such influences from the opposite house or 120° are not described in this book.

A1. The Emperor (紫微)

AUTHORITATIVE, PIONEERING, CONQUERING, FAR-SIGHTED, HOT TEMPERED

IN THE SELF HOUSE

The self is a strong individual with an expanded view on life's phenomena. This person is able to view problems or challenges from all angles and is not afraid to take chances. He takes action. There will also be a lot of idle talk surrounding. The Emperor represents the head, either the CEO of an organization or encountering events/ injuries having to do with the head.

IN THE ELDERS HOUSE	Clients, parents or those above you will be strong-willed and unyielding. The key word here would be patience – in dealing with these people.
IN KARMIC WEALTH	The Self is strong-willed and a fighter.
IN THE PROPERTIES HOUSE	The Self resides on high ground, or on the upper floors in a high-rise building. If the self is a business owner, the company deals with power and action.
IN THE CAREER HOUSE	The Self holds down a job that enjoys autonomy and has a say in the running of the business.
IN THE STAFF HOUSE	Confident and strong employees. These will be independent workers.
IN THE TRAVEL HOUSE	Indicates a turn for the better after migrating to a foreign land.
IN THE HEALTH SECTOR	Problems with the head, spleen or stomach areas.
IN THE PROSPERITY HOUSE	The Self deals with, or possesses power in financial matters. Does not necessarily indicate a prosperous Self, e.g. careers in financial control, money management, etc.

IN THE MINORS HOUSE	Strong, confident children or senior employees.
IN THE SPOUSE HOUSE	A stronger spouse than the self.
IN THE PEERS HOUSE	Business associates or siblings are stronger and more powerful than the self. Siblings or partners number between two to three.

A2. Intelligence (天機)

STRATEGY, PIONEERING, MOVEMENTS (LATERAL), MECHANICS, AGILITY

IN THE SELF SECTOR	The self is quick-witted, has an agile mind and is prone to change.
IN THE ELDERS SECTOR	A lot is going with clients, parents or those above you. Schemes are in the air.
IN KARMIC WEALTH	Heavy thoughts occupy the Self.
IN PROPERTIES	Much movement surrounds your place of residence e.g. do you live near a busy road or junction, or machinery plant?
IN THE CAREER SECTOR	Much on-the-job traveling will be involved. Strategic planning and innovative ideas are your forte.

IN THE STAFF HOUSE	Changes among employees. Those in employment by you will be required to, or excel in, strategic analyzing.
IN THE TRAVEL HOUSE	You will be kept busy, physically as well as mentally, after migrating to a foreign land.
IN THE HEALTH SECTOR	Ailments having to do with the limbs, liver or bile areas.
IN PROSPERITY	This is a year of busy financial transactions.
IN THE MINORS SECTOR	The children face danger. An indication of a miscarriage or abortion. Do not discount abductions. Those under you (or your children) are forward-thinking and smart. Employees will be involved in much travel.
IN THE SPOUSE SECTOR	Much traveling is involved for the spouse. This is a time for endings, separations and divorce. The Spouse has a quick mind and often comes up with innovative ideas.
IN THE PEERS SECTOR	Business associates or siblings may come and go. Some scheming may be going on.

A3. The Sun (太陽)

BENEVOLENCE, YANG, MASCULINITY, OPENNESS, STATUS, ELEGANCE

IN THE SELF SECTOR

The Sun in the Self for Tiger, Rabbit and Dragon sectors will be basking in the limelight – you won't fail to notice this person. He will also love to give a helping hand. A careful individual who is also prone to extravagance.

IN THE ELDERS SECTOR

Much controversy surrounds your elders or employers/clients. These individuals will be involved with broadcasting, light, lighting, transmission or transport.

IN KARMIC WEALTH

The Self will be more of a dreamer than an implementer. Problems would occur should real steps be taken for the dream to be formed into reality.

IN THE PROPERTIES SECTOR

In the Home Sector or falling in the Tiger, Rabbit or Dragon houses, the home will be bright and sunny. If in business, it will have to do with broadcasting, light, lighting, or transmission or transport.

IN THE CAREER SECTOR	Your career has to do with light, lighting or the transmission/communication or transportation professions.
IN THE STAFF SECTOR	Superficiality amongst employees. Guard against confidential matters coming to light through employees.
IN THE TRAVEL SECTOR	Fame comes after migration to a foreign land.
IN THE HEALTH SECTOR	Has to do with the head, heart and eyes areas.
IN THE PROSPERITY SECTOR	The Sun in the Prosperity Sector stands for fame more than for monetary gains. In this sector, the Self may attain fame because of his involvement with the rich and famous.
IN THE MINORS SECTOR	Children or employees will be helpful, in the public eye and enjoy a measure of recognition. There is a tendency for miscarriages or abortions.
IN THE SPOUSE SECTOR	The spouse will be involved in some benevolent, public activities. A reputable figure.
IN THE PEERS SECTOR	Business associates or siblings will be in the public eye. There will be around three to four siblings or partners.

A4. The Commander (武曲)

WEALTH, LEADERSHIP, ENTREPRENEURIAL SKILLS, HANDICRAFTS, METALS

IN THE SELF SECTOR

The physical Self will be slightly built with a resounding, resonant voice. The individual is a craftsman and an implementer, involved with the nuts and bolts of putting an idea to work.

IN THE ELDERS SECTOR

Clients, parents or those above you will be strong-willed and unyielding. The key word here would be patience – in dealing with these people. These people will deal in one form of craft or another.

IN KARMIC WEALTH

The Self is strong-willed and a fighter.

IN THE PROPERTIES SECTOR

The Self resides near metal e.g. the home is decorated with metals, or a martial arts center.

IN THE CAREER SECTOR

The Self holds down a job that enjoys autonomy and has a say in the running of the business.

IN THE STAFF SECTOR

There are confident and strong employees working for you.

IN THE TRAVEL SECTOR	The Commander here indicates much hectic activities after migrating to a foreign land.
IN THE HEALTH SECTOR	Ailments with the lung area. The Commander has to do with metals – which relates to injuries by metals or surgeries.
IN THE PROSPERITY SECTOR	The Self deals with, or possesses power in financial matters. This does not necessarily indicate a prosperous Self, e.g. careers in financial control, money management, etc. The surrounding stars give a fuller picture.
IN THE MINORS SECTOR	Strong, confident children or senior employees.
IN THE SPOUSE SECTOR	The spouse will be small and demure with a resonant voice – the stronger of the pair.
IN THE PEERS SECTOR	Business associates or siblings will be blunt, straightforward individuals. They produce fast, methodical results.

A5. The Waif (天同)

EMOTIONAL, ENJOYMENT, SENSITIVITY, GENTLENESS, BUILDING FROM NOTHING

IN THE SELF SECTOR

The Waif here brings in emotional volatility, and a hard childhood. She will be fair, has a squarish-round face and round shoulders. She possesses the ability to build wealth from nothing. So, watch out for this one – especially if auspicious, bright stars surround.

IN THE ELDERS SECTOR

Clients, parents or those above you will be emotional and their help is but limited.

IN KARMIC WEALTH

The Waif does well if found in Karmic Wealth. She has the ability to build from nothing. However, if surrounded by the dark stars, she could be easily influenced. In which case – a strong, calm exterior tends to hide an emotional self.

IN PROPERTIES

The Self will have experienced upheavals in the family in the early years. The present home is on low ground or the lower levels of a building.

IN THE CAREER SECTOR   The Self holds down a career in the arts, entertainment or any area that The Waif's graciousness can be put to the fore.

IN THE STAFF SECTOR   The Waif in this house begets weak, uninspired employees.

IN THE TRAVEL SECTOR   An indication of a turn for the worse after migrating or traveling in a foreign land. With dark stars surrounding, watch out for mishaps at times of play.

IN THE HEALTH SECTOR   Heavy stuff to handle having to do with the emotions! The kidneys or reproductive systems will also be causes for concern.

IN THE PROSPERITY SECTOR   A certain fortune will be lost and there will be several phases where there is just not enough funding to go around.

IN THE MINORS SECTOR   The Self will enjoy a strong, positive relationship with children or senior employees. However, the children will be weak.

IN THE SPOUSE SECTOR   The spouse is often in emotional turmoil which will lead to unhappiness in the relationship.

IN THE PEERS SECTOR   Business associates or siblings relationship will be satisfactory. However, these persons will not be of great help. There will be 3-4 partners or siblings.

A6. *Crimson* (廉貞)

BLOOD RELATIONS, EMOTIONAL ISSUES, ARTS, POLITICS, PRIVACY, FEMININE

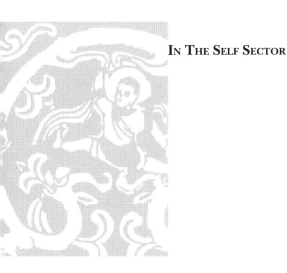

IN THE SELF SECTOR   Flirtatious and sociable, The Self will, however, closely guard his privacy. She will be strong emotionally and quite intuitive. This individual is an artist by nature and just loves being surrounded by art, music, theatre and the like. She can deftly weave her influence and reach his goals with dexterity. A splendidly munificent personality.

IN THE ELDERS SECTOR Masked by an outwardly friendly nature, clients, parents or those above you will be hard to gauge.

IN KARMIC WEALTH The Self guards her privacy well.

IN THE PROPERTIES SECTOR Crimson having to do with *Yin*, the female element, The Self may live near females or the residential area will be dark and shady. May live near blood, the theatre or an artistic community.

IN THE CAREER SECTOR Those with Crimson in the Career Sector will do famously well in situations which require constant dealings with the opposite sex. Look for situations where you can bask in attention, for therein lies your success.

IN THE STAFF SECTOR Distrustful employees.

IN THE TRAVEL SECTOR Indicates an accident and bloodshed after migrating to a foreign land. Also, emotional attachments or problems may surface. Secrecy in the Travel Sector may point to involvement with illegal immigration.

IN THE HEALTH SECTOR Pain and psychological problems. Being prone to ailments having to do with the blood, Crimson will also bring in major illnesses.

IN THE PROSPERITY SECTOR The Self deals with financial matters with blood relatives. These are kept under wraps.

IN THE MINORS SECTOR Children and senior employees tend to keep matters to themselves. It is imperative to keep an open dialogue at all times.

IN THE SPOUSE SECTOR The spouse is dealing with emotional problems or is keeping a secret. The blood element is strong – having to do with illness or an operation.

IN THE PEERS SECTOR Business associates, siblings or the competitor will have one or two things up their sleeve. There will be two to three siblings or partners in business. However, Crimson in this sector points to death, either in vitro or at a very young age. Alternatively – adoption.

A7. The Vault (天府)

PROSPERITY, POSSESSIONS, PRESERVATION, CAREFULNESS, INTEGRITY

IN THE SELF SECTOR

The Self will be careful and detailed. His parents and elders will play an important part in forming his character and personality and ultimately, his success later on in life. It is a characteristic of the Vault that this individual will not lack for earthly possessions.

IN THE ELDERS SECTOR

The General (A13) in the opposite sector brings great changes and upheavals to clients, parents or those above. The Vault in the Elders Sector inevitably brings in The Scholar (A12) in the Self Sector. This stands for helpful, loving and supportive parents.

IN KARMIC WEALTH

The Vault in the Karmic Sector inevitably has General in the Self Sector. These two apparently contradicting personalities form a person who thirsts for stability (The Vault) but is actually experiencing constant turbulence and changes (The General).

IN THE PROPERTIES SECTOR The Self resides on low ground, or on the lower floors of an apartment building. He is likely to remain in one location for a very long time.

IN THE CAREER SECTOR The Self holds down a steady job. Although this may mean security, this may also be lacking in spark and creativity.

IN THE STAFF SECTOR Stable employees whom you can count on. However, by the same token, they lack flexibility.

IN THE TRAVEL SECTOR With The General (A13) in the opposite sector (The Self), this indicates a blow after migrating to a foreign land.

IN THE HEALTH SECTOR Concerned with the stomach, ribs or lung areas.

IN THE PROSPERITY SECTOR The Self will have to deal with problems arising where money matters are concerned.

IN THE MINORS SECTOR Weak, sickly children. The Self takes to heart his influence on his children or senior employees.

IN THE SPOUSE SECTOR The spouse will be conservative and cautious. The General in the opposite sector would have brought on some form of failure for the spouse or loved one, which will reflect as a difficult lesson in life.

IN THE PEERS SECTOR

Don't expect much support or help from business associates or siblings. Because The General will always be in the opposite sector, this star will bring on some form of failure for siblings, business associates or the competition.

18. The Moon (太陰)

NIGHT, FEMININE, TRANQUILITY, RETIRING, GRACEFUL, WEALTH

IN THE SELF SECTOR

The Wealth part of the Chinese character for Abundance, The Moon in The Self sector makes for a wealthy individual. A lukewarm relationship with the female parent during one's formative years. A woman with a brilliant Moon in her Self sector will be beautiful, romantic, a homemaker and very supportive of her spouse and family.

IN THE ELDERS SECTOR

Parents, clients and seniors are quiet, retiring wealthy individuals.

IN KARMIC WEALTH

The Self will spend much time in solitude contemplation. A deep, wise individual with a colorful imagination.

IN THE PROPERTIES SECTOR The Self resides near water and there is likely to be woodland surrounding. You will prefer blues or greens as your interior colors.

IN THE CAREER SECTOR The Self holds down a career which has to do with women or feminine interests, finance, or be working into the night.

IN THE STAFF SECTOR Steady employees who work quietly and effectively for your benefit.

IN THE TRAVEL SECTOR If migrating to a foreign land, tranquility will follow.

IN THE HEALTH SECTOR The Self will be concerned with psychological unrest, the kidneys or reproductive areas. Ailments having to do with water.

IN THE PROSPERITY SECTOR The Self will be able to accumulate savings or a nest egg in the long run. Note this is the general source of wealth for this individual.

IN THE MINORS SECTOR Children or senior employees tend to be quiet or retiring.

IN THE SPOUSE SECTOR A retiring spouse or loved one who will be wealthy in her own right.

IN THE PEERS SECTOR Siblings, business associates or the competition are retiring. Three to four siblings or business associates.

A9. Opportunity (貪狼)

INDULGENCE, SENSUOUSNESS, PHYSIQUE, MUSCLES, SPORTS, DIVINATION

IN THE SELF SECTOR

You enjoy sports or any form of physical activity and may delve into the intricacies of other-worldly knowledge. You won't be out of place at any party or social function. An opportunist to the core, there will be many sets of friends from different social backgrounds.

IN THE ELDERS SECTOR

Parents, clients and seniors are at their most charming. However, you will not be close to these people.

IN KARMIC WEALTH

Opportunity in the Karmic Sector inevitably has The Vault (A7) in the Self. Coming to terms with these apparently contradicting personalities will be the cause for inner conflicts. The steady character of The Vault will constantly be called upon to deal with the decadent pursuits of Opportunity.

IN THE PROPERTIES SECTOR

You reside near sports grounds or entertainment establishments. If in business, your success comes with entertainment, socializing, sports and other physical activities, or meeting with many different people.

IN THE CAREER SECTOR   The Self holds down a career which requires constant entertaining.

IN THE STAFF SECTOR   Be wary of employees who has developed some form of vice or addiction which could affect your interests.

IN THE TRAVEL SECTOR   Look for Bell or Fire in the same or opposite sector or at 120°. These are supportive stars and will bring in some good opportunities when traveling or after having migrated to another land.

IN THE HEALTH SECTOR   The Self will be concerned with liver or bile problems. Muscular problems.

IN THE PROSPERITY SECTOR   A brilliant Opportunity with Fire (C25) make a dynamic duo. These two stars join to create power and prosperity. Alone in this sector, Opportunity will still make her mark.

IN THE MINORS SECTOR   Sports, body-training or any physical pursuits will interest these people. The youngsters are charming and sociable. You will enjoy their many interests.

IN THE SPOUSE SECTOR	A charming spouse or loved one with many interests. She will be active and have an interest in divination.
IN THE PEERS SECTOR	Be wary of friends or associates developing vested interests of some form or another.

A10. The Messenger (巨門)

SLANDER, LITIGATION, CAREFULNESS, PRIVACY, SUSPICION, LARGENESS

IN THE SELF SECTOR	A person who is careful and detailed. The Messenger also stands for events developing under the surface, the undercurrent. Things may not be what they seem. Depending on adjacent stars, The Messenger may eradicate bad influences or bring dissatisfaction to the surface. Before you know what hit you – it's a done deal.
IN THE ELDERS SECTOR	Parents, clients and seniors are prone to quarreling among themselves.
IN KARMIC WEALTH	An individual engaging in intricate

details and disquieting thoughts. Not one of your happy-go-lucky types.

IN THE PROPERTIES SECTOR The Self resides on low ground which may also be dark and shady; or the lower floors of an apartment building. The home may be near a courtroom – where much talking and disputes take place. Or it could be just near eating establishments – anything having to do with the mouth.

IN THE CAREER SECTOR The Self holds down a career in public relations, marketing or selling – using the voice.

IN THE STAFF SECTOR Be aware that employees will be prone to slander or litigation. These will be careful people and, depending on the influence of other stars, will be verbally gifted or aggravatingly discourteous to customers.

IN THE TRAVEL SECTOR You experience much slander, idle talk or litigation after moving to another country. You will also engage in somewhat secretive activities.

Tarnished reputation and credibility

IN THE HEALTH SECTOR Problems developing in or around the mouth area.

IN THE PROSPERITY SECTOR Slanders occurring from financial or money matters, litigation. On the other hand, a secret financial gain.

IN THE MINORS SECTOR There is much disagreements and talking among children or senior employees. This could also stand for these individuals being linguistically endowed. However, in the presence of unsympathetic stars, the opposite will be true.

IN THE SPOUSE SECTOR You will drawn into verbal disagreements with your loved one.

IN THE PEERS SECTOR Be wary of friends or associates engaging in slander or disagreements among themselves.

A11. The Mirror (天相)

Leverage? REPEATING, HELPFULNESS, RESPONSIBILITY, INFLUENCE, EMBROILMENT

IN THE SELF SECTOR

As the Mirror reflects, so the Self is repeated. An indication of a twin, whether identical or not. This is a helpful individual who goes out of this way in aid of others. Whether it would be influencing good or embroiling in the bad, this individual loves to get involved. Always reflecting The Pioneer (A14) in its opposite (Prosperity) sector, the individual strives to bring in great changes. However, because of what he is, he may tend to repeat past endeavors. Break out of the circle and he moves forward.

IN THE ELDERS SECTOR

A duplication of parents? Absurd as this may sound, in ancient China, this takes on the meaning of concubines. In the West – godparents.

IN KARMIC WEALTH

Duo characters struggle within and disquieting thoughts repeat themselves. This is where 'embroiling' comes in to play. Learn to acknowledge and gently admonish these to achieve peace of mind.

IN THE PROPERTIES SECTOR   The Self lives in a duplex-style house or at the annex of a residence. Mirrors reflect their influence in the home. This sector reflects the business – an indication of subsidiaries. Also, the obvious – two family homes. The various meanings for this would have to be confirmed by other stars.

IN THE CAREER SECTOR   The Self holds down a career in the service industries, printing or duplicating business. Having to do with paper, translation or editing processes.

IN THE STAFF SECTOR   Your employees perform duo roles, overseeing diverging interests or different departments for you. Be also aware of two-faced characters. Rivalry between different factors or departments.

IN THE TRAVEL SECTOR   Mirror in the Travel Sector will always be reflected by The Pioneer (A14) in its opposite Self sector. An indication that there will be more new lands to conquer. This is not one to stay long in one place.

IN THE HEALTH SECTOR   Illnesses with the ability to spread and infect; or hereditary diseases. Diseases which have to do with water or the skin surface.

IN THE PROSPERITY SECTOR   Depending on influencing stars, good things come in doubles. However, the same goes for bad influences. Other stars in the same or opposing sector give insights.

IN THE MINORS SECTOR   Duplicating i.e. twins or an indication of premature birth.

IN THE SPOUSE SECTOR   More than one love interest at the same time or that the spouse is one's opposite i.e. physically, coming from a totally different background – in education or culture. Or, the union developing from a different relationship from the past i.e. distant cousins, former classmates, colleagues, etc.

IN THE PEERS SECTOR   The Mirror in this sector indicates many siblings – including the self, five or above. Among these individuals who are twins, dual characters and the like. The Mirror stands for repeating; therefore you meet up with people from the past and these become your partners in business. Regarding rivals – a disagreement between parties or groups of people.

A12. The Scholar (天梁)

PROTECTION, LONGEVITY, LATENESS, SOLITUDE, CONTROLING, LITIGATION

IN THE SELF SECTOR

The Self will always be protected or feel a sense of protection by the influence of The Scholar. This is also a longevity star – pointing the way to a long, albeit lonesome existence. The Self may find himself in trouble with the law. Others shun or keep a certain distance from this him. The Self will be disciplined and principled. He is associated with medicines or medication.

IN THE ELDERS SECTOR

A significant age difference between the parents and the Self or the Self is born late into the marriage.

IN KARMIC WEALTH

The individual is blessed with a superior memory. Not geared to impulsive actions, his movements will be slow and deliberate. He has set his ways and that's the way it will be.

IN THE PROPERTIES SECTOR

The Self is likely to remain in one home for a long time. The family home will be near a retirement home, an old establishment or a hospital.

IN THE CAREER SECTOR	The Self holds down a career in the traditional services, medicine or medication fields. A slow development – whatever that may be involved. Patience will be the keyword, which points to accountancy. You may also be drawn to the disciplinary forces.
IN THE STAFF SECTOR	Your employees tend to be slow-acting and set in their ways. Often, these will be long-standing employees who have spent a lifetime with you.
IN THE TRAVEL SECTOR	Problems will surface after migrating to a foreign land. However, this person usually stays put after making this move.
IN THE HEALTH SECTOR	Long-standing illnesses, developing slowly. Males – illnesses relating to the stomach area. Females – the breasts.
IN THE PROSPERITY SECTOR	Disputes, unrest brought on by earnings.
IN THE MINORS SECTOR	The late arrival of children in the marriage. Or, the maturity of the children greatly surpasses their age.
IN THE SPOUSE SECTOR	A substantial age difference between

partners and/or a marriage after a long courtship.

IN THE PEERS SECTOR

The Scholar in this sector indicates an abundance of siblings or partners, with substantial age differences in between – five years and upwards.

A13. The General (七殺)

SEVERITY, STRATEGY, INDEPENDENCE, ALOOFNESS, STAGNANT, HESITATION

IN THE SELF SECTOR

A quiet, sturdy individual who likes to walk alone. Blessed with a general's fortitude, he is strong and independent. However, little does he know he needs all the help he can get. Few words fall from his lips but nothing escapes his sharp gaze. A physical trait – lush body hair. A sharp blow at a young age comes with The General in the Self. With supporting stars to help him out, he rides the wave and emerge the better for it.

IN THE ELDERS SECTOR

Parents, seniors or clients will be bad-tempered. This totally perplexes you.

Hard lessons await these people.

IN KARMIC WEALTH

The General in the Karmic Sector will inevitably have The Mirror (A11) in its opposite, Prosperity. An indication of inner turmoil. A poet by nature, he indulges in much deep thought. A lonesome individual.

IN THE PROPERTIES SECTOR

Very independent and self-contained, The Self is likely to live in a freestanding house. No high-rises or apartments for this one. Schools or colleges will be nearby.

IN THE CAREER SECTOR

Whether holding down a job or not, the Self will enjoy being his own boss. Much independence is called for and he will relish every moment of it. The General in your Career sector gives you much power – so go for it!

IN THE STAFF SECTOR

Those under you will be independent and comes with a strong temper. Look out for these hot-headed individuals. Otherwise, hard lessons will have to be learned.

IN THE TRAVEL SECTOR

The General in the Travel Sector will always be reflected by The Vault in its opposite (Self) sector. This combination indicates certain difficult lessons to be learned in the throes of change. This has to do with the difficult dance of the Vault (safe and traditional) partnering the General (daring and individualistic).

IN THE HEALTH SECTOR   Illnesses of the lungs; breathing or problems of the digestive track. Injuries to the rib-cage area.

IN THE PROSPERITY SECTOR   Disputes and unrest brought on by earnings.

IN THE MINORS SECTOR   Strong children who says little of what is going on inside. Alas, there will be many lessons to be learned.

IN THE SPOUSE SECTOR   Silent and independent, your partner will prove to be perplexing and difficult. Hard lessons for your loved one has to be learned.

IN THE PEERS SECTOR   You will have problems getting siblings or partners to communicate. The General brings a hard lesson for these people.

A14. *The Pioneer* (破軍)

OUT WITH THE OLD, IN WITH THE NEW, HOPE, PIONEERING, HOT TEMPERED

IN THE SELF SECTOR — With The Mirror (A11) in its opposite sector, this pair brings much changes throughout life. The Pioneer in the Self may sport a scar. This is a strong individual who is also a rebel – the marks of a true pioneer. A mover by nature, he will not be content to stay put in one spot for long. The Mirror influences twins – or a sibling/partner resembling a twin soul. The young Pioneer, however, will be quite a sickly child early on in life.

IN THE ELDERS SECTOR — You have more than the conventional one set of parents. Clients or parents are self-starters – either in their own businesses or just being very forward-thinking in their own right.

IN KARMIC WEALTH — The mind fills with new, inventive, pioneering ideas. You are a busy, innovative self who inspires others.

IN THE PROPERTIES SECTOR — The very modern, state-of-the-art kind, 'intelligent' kind of dwelling would most likely appeal to you.

IN THE CAREER SECTOR — You will be out there at the forefront of any new industry. Moreover, you'll be wearing different hats, as befitting the circumstance.

IN THE STAFF SECTOR — Independent, even rebellious people under you. Be mindful that these individuals do not annoy customers and clients.

IN THE TRAVEL SECTOR — The Pioneer in the Travel Sector indicates someone who loves to travel and settle in foreign lands. This will be an on-going trait throughout life.

IN THE HEALTH SECTOR — There will be a hidden illness which shows up in its late state. Study the Mirror (A11) in its Karmic Wealth sector for more insight.

IN THE PROSPERITY SECTOR — An exceedingly creative individual when it comes to finding his fortunes.

IN THE MINORS SECTOR — The eldest child bears the blow. Indications of premature birth or complications, a sickly childhood and/or scarring. Active, rebellious children.

IN THE SPOUSE SECTOR — The partners will be different as night and day. Discarding the old for the new is the Pioneer's main trait. There will be at least two marriages.

IN THE PEERS SECTOR — The eldest child bears the heaviest burden, in the form of illnesses. Age differences among the children will be great. Other distinctive differences include education, intelligence or their stations in life. The Mirror opposite the Self will bring a twin or a pair of exceptionally close siblings — twin souls. This is family of rebels.

4 The Auspicious Stars *8 stars*

If set right by the brilliant auspicious stars, they enhance their wonderful powers, making for an even more successful sector.

These eight stars love to bestow their many blessings and they have but a few slight dents. If set right by the brilliant, auspicious stars, they enhance their wonderful powers, making for an even more successful sector. Should these find themselves in the presence of the evil or major stars in retrograde, they have the power to weaken the damage. If helped by a brilliant major star, an auspicious star can even turn the damage around and bring out the good qualities of an albeit evil star. However, their healing powers will be weak if made to stand alone in any sector.

The *pairing* of these stars are essential if their full benevolent influence is to be brought forth. Whether these are to be found in the same house, at opposites or 120°, the following three pairs depend on each other to shine:

The Left and Right Ministers (B15 & B16)
The Literary and Art Ministers (B17 & B18)
Stardust and Delight (B19 & B20)

B15. The Left Minister (左輔)

This star stands for honor, kindness and acceptance. The Left Minister in the Self sector makes for an attractive individual who is calm and elegant. He will be striving for the best – literally reaching for the stars. Always the optimist, he can safely see himself through any crisis. However, he needn't worry too much about bad luck – he has the innate ability to ward this off. This is one star which possesses the most karmic wealth.

Acceptance being one of his trademarks, the Left Minister takes hard work and responsibility in his stride and will be kept busy. The Left Minister enhances all the other stars. However, should he meet up with a dark Ram, Fire, or Bell, his powers will be dimmed.

The Left Minister's one weakness will be brought to the fore if placed in the Spouse's sector. A rocky marriage, for sure – should it be teamed with dark or evil stars. The Left Minister in the Minors sector indicates few children (one or at the most two) or these coming very late in life.

B16. The Right Minister (右弼)

*T*he other supporting arm to the Emperor, this is a Glowing star with qualities very similar to The Left Minister.

Its powers are, however, dimmer than that of the Left Minister and with a major difference - it trails matters of the sexual or seductive kind. However, associations brought on by this star do not last. Accept the pain as part and parcel. Watch out for a pairing up with The Scholar (A12), The Child (A5), Intelligence (A2), The Messenger (A10) or The Commander (A4) in the same house, its opposite or at 120°. Such a liaison spells disaster of the romantic kind – a relationship doomed to end, but not without its long drawn out theatrics first of all.

The Right Minister in the Spouse sector indicates incompatibility, sadness and upheavals, finally ending in separation.

B17. *Literary Minister* (文昌)

T his star has to do with literary matters, education, the arts and major examinations. Alone in the Self sector and in its Brilliant stage, this star makes an attractive individual who is charming, knowledgeable and refined in the arts. She would also be outstanding, both in demeanor and literary accomplishments. Joined by other Brilliants, you'd definitely be getting a head-turner!

The best pairing up for the Literary Minister would be with The Sun (A3) or Scholar (A12). If joined by Completion (A22), the perfect but very rare quad-angled star combination of beauty, brains and outstanding accomplishment will be formed. Such a combination would be in the birth chart of star-quality, high-profile individuals. The opposite sex's attraction to them is inevitable. She will have many admirers throughout life. A thought for comfort is: this minister has her head firmly screwed on and any romantic pursuit that she lets herself be drawn into, she makes sure becomes a lasting, beautiful affair.

The Literary Minister excels in public examinations and goes on to holding public offices of high stature and success. This star shines in education, the arts or media. You will hear about them.

B18. *The Arts Minister* (文曲)

Not unlike the Literary Minister, our Arts Minister in the Self sector is equally attractive, elegant and refined. This refinement is however applied to self-expression – music, oratorical pursuits, the performing arts. Spiritual matters would also intrigue this individual and she would be drawn to turn to the stars to find her answers. The road less traveled is for her and it would be by bravely treading where few has gone before that this Minister will find her way and ultimate reward.

Either of these two Ministers, if found in the Self sector, make for very interesting company. In their brilliant hours, aided by other brilliants, these individuals are heart-breakingly attractive to the opposite sex. Unfortunately, this one is too artsy for her own good and any romantic pursuit will bring about much chagrin and unhappiness.

B19. Stardust (天魁)

A delightfully helpful star to have in any sector of the birth chart. Especially in the Self sector, as long as the major stars have some measure of brightness and there are no inauspicious stars around, the whole lifetime can be enhanced by Stardust. Expect the appearance of helpful individuals in various periods of the life in aid of your pursuits – mentors during formative years, sympathetic job interviewers, supportive managers at work, etc. Note that where Stardust shines, luck seeks you out – a timely, helping hand. There's no need to look for these helpful souls because, let's face it, you won't be able to recognize them in the moment. You will remember Stardust in retrospect.

A point to remember, though. After age 50 Stardust goes into Retrograde and becomes the opponent. From this point on, Stardust stagnates and blocks.

A20. Delight (天鉞)

Another helpful little twinkler that guides, protects and points one in the right direction in the guise of helpful individuals. The difference from Stardust is that this star comes with delightfully exciting contacts with the opposite sex. Love may grow from *sympatique.*

Where there is a possibility that you may not recognize Stardust, you will definitely miss Delight. Delight works incognito!

As with Stardust, after age 50, Delight goes into Retrograde and begins to work against you. A good reason to go into early retirement? You bet, but remember to reap your rewards early on.

B21. The Winged Horse (天馬)

A powerful stallion that flies across the skies with grace and fortitude. A busy individual – in fact, the busier, the better. The rewards of his toils will be sooner felt. A different personality from The General (A13) and The Pioneer (A14) who deal with innovation and pioneering with much upheaval, the Winged Horse, whilst shining on bright achievers, brings none of the upheavals associated with great changes.

Look for the Winged Horse at any of the four extremities in the birth chart. You will only find him at one of the four corner houses and none other.

The Winged Horse, being a twinkling star at its brightest, is not strong enough in itself to exert much power. With the help of Completion (A22), the pair fuels each other to a brilliant success. The Winged Horse/Completion pair indicates success coming from faraway, business travel, or emigrating.

Brilliant stars from its opposite house and the adjacent 120° two houses also have the affect of uplifting the Winged Horse. These include The Emperor (A1), The Vault (A7), The Moon (A8), Opportunity (A9), The Minister (A11) and Completion

(A22). Again, these combinations indicate reaping rewards through traveling or working abroad. Expect recognition being part and parcel of this success.

However, if teamed with The Pioneer (A14) or Intelligence (A2), the indication is for an exhaustive road ahead for an extremely clever and agile individual. The reward factor, too, would be diminished. Faced with any of the dark stars and the Winged Horse will encounter accidents or danger whilst on the road.

Many a times, the Winged Horse will settle in the Spouse sector. The husband can expect unswerving support from his wife, or the lady will be independently wealthy. If you are a woman, you can always depend on your husband to look out for your career or aid him in his.

If you have the Winged Horse in your Self or opposite sector, or at 120° both directions, answer that beckoning from beyond the horizon, and start packing! Success awaits you there.

B22. Completion (祿存)

A glowing, lucky star that brings material and spiritual wealth as well as having the ability to avert danger. A definite enhancer to any of the major stars, it brings the good to new heights and thwarts the detrimental powers of the dark stars.

Completion in the Self house makes for an upright, honest individual with a big heart. This star indicates a rewarding lifetime of wealth and prosperity without the rigmaroles of toils, hardships or great changes.

The wealth that Completion brings carries its own peculiarity in that it never stops. You don't have to work (too much) for it; you don't inherit it. In fact, you don't think about it much, but there it is! Even in the same sector as the dark stars, it doesn't quite dry up.

You will not find this star in the sectors of the Dog, Ox, Dragon or Goat. Its orbit is such that it never enters these sectors. The other distinction about Completion is that where it is located, it is always hemmed in by the Spinning Top in the immediate sector behind and Ram in front, the two dark stars. Consequently, you will never find Completion and these stars sharing the same sector. Well, that's two trouble-makers out of the way, at least you may think. Perhaps, but not quite ...

Should Completion sit alone in one sector, hemmed in by the Spinning Top and Ram before and after, these dark stars deplete its source and, quashed by these, Completion will never really become very wealthy – spiritually or materially. But then again, how much is enough?

A lone Completion in a sector indicates an overly defensive, miserly and lonesome individual who believes in no one but himself. Spurned by others, much hardship and dispute surround, mostly involving his hard-earned money.

Where Completions falls into any 10-year period or particular year is an indication for added protection or prosperity. This is also a healing star – it heralds a new beginning where past hurts or losses can finally be put to rest.

Completion also has its own way to deal with the dark stars. Its mere presence is enough to render useless their powers.

5 The Dark Stars

6 stars
C23 - C28

If latched onto a weak major star, they have the power to poison. Alas, these dark stars are a necessity in life's journey …

As their name suggests, these six stars forebode setback and even life threatening situations. A Dark Star sharing the same sector with a Brilliant is unfortunate, as it would have the power to deplete any fine characteristics the Brilliant might bring.

If latched onto a weak major star, they have the power to poison. Alas, these dark stars are a necessity in life's journey as it is through these murky days that we learn the most. We are then propelled to greater success. In your darkest hours, remember this: Our worst enemies are in fact our greatest teachers.

A major characteristic that all the Dark Stars share would be Anger. Do not let it consume. Use anger as a propellant. A positively angry person would be a hard-boiled, no-nonsense individual who applies anger as ammunition for her goals.

Women with a lone dark star (with the exception of The Ram) in their Self house will have a hard childhood; but (perhaps as compensation!) grow up to become a rare, exceptional beauty. A man with this occurrence will, through much hardship and toil, be able to establish his own business and eventually go on to build an empire.

C23. *The Ram* (擎羊)

Often referred to as a flying spear, this star brings life-threatening accidents or attacks. An dangerous star, the Ram destroys or weakens the good stars and at the same time constrains the other dark stars with the exception of Fire. The Ram in the Self sector or directly opposite, whether male or female, indicates a serious accident at an early age, the affects of which will be lifelong. Healing will be lengthy, or the individual just learns to live with this shadow. Look for the brilliant or auspicious stars which will counteract the damage.

The Ram in the self sector which happens to fall into either the Dragon, Ox, Sheep or Dog chambers makes for an individual who is open, up-front and a bit of a rebel. Such a man will be distinguished looking. The female, if free of other dark stars in the Self, will also be enticingly beautiful. This accounts for a brilliant Ram. The brilliant Ram brings in propitious surprises. If met up with Fire, sparks fly and these two can make things happen.

The Ram with The Waif (A5) or the The Moon (A8) in the Horse chamber would boost the energy of these two rather weak stars and propel them to great heights.

C24. *The Spinning Top* (陀羅)

I f the Ram is the flying spear, the Spinning Top would be the hidden arrows. This does not bring in dangers of the life threatening kind. It hurts by initiating idle talk and gossips, loneliness in old age, delays (in career success or marriage) or separations – leaving of the family home at a young age. In its dark state, these blockages will be enhanced. If found with Fire, Bell, the Void or Punishment in the same sector, the Spinning Top then acts as a catalyst to bring out these stars' positive traits.

The Spinning Top brings the least destruction among the Dark Stars. This is especially so in its Brilliant state (when it is in the chambers of the Dragon, Ram, Dog and Ox) and in the presence of Brilliant or Auspicious stars

C25. *Fire* (火星)

A roaring individual who will not be constrained, leaving chaos and destruction at its wake. In the Self sector, this dark star hones a fiery temper and a strong, often unyielding personality. If left unchecked in the absence of positive, brilliant stars, it brings tragic catastrophes at an early age. At the same level, this can mean a name-change brought on by the early death of the father and the mother remarries. Fire also brings physical impairments.

Although a dark star by nature, Fire can be toned down by some brilliant, major stars. One of these would be The General (A13) – our action hero, who is on a par with Fire's awesome strength. This pair in the Self sector increases the burden. Your road to success will not be smooth.

A brilliant Fire when paired with Ram in any sector is a good sign. Each not only cancels out the other's destruction, they also go on to manifest extraordinary pioneering qualities. However, much hard work will be involved.

The best combination with Fire would be with a brilliant Opportunity (A9). These two stars join to create power and prosperity.

No matter male or female, a lone Fire in the Self sector indicates an outstanding, successful achiever. The best scenario? Call in the The Emperor (A1) or his Left and Right Ministers (B15 & B16) or the angelic beings, Stardust (B19) and Delight (B20).

Fire is a major disruptive star and, apart from the above, brings out the worst in any star. Look for the Auspicious stars or the Brilliants at its opposite sector or 120° either side. Without these, Fire would bring in huge and rapid rewards and before you can say 'poof', it's all gone up in smoke!

C26. *The Bell* (鈴星)

A less formidable star than Fire, but nevertheless a force to be reckoned with. Without the benevolent rays of The Emperor (A1), Opportunity (A9), or The General (A13) the Bell in the Self sector indicates a hard cataclysmic childhood and this lonesome individual will grow up crusty and tough. As with Fire, there are indications of a name-change (e.g. adoption) and crippling injuries.

Bell and Fire, being similar in nature, very often work together. A sector, if flanked by these two stars immediately before and after it, will be especially weak. These stars also lend strength to each other should they be placed directly at opposite ends. The Self sector, if without strong, brilliant stars and hemmed in by Bell and Fire, indicates a life fraught with difficulties however much one might try.

C27. The Void (地空) *Also Extraordinary ideas*
P. 165—

This major dark star works against anything having to do with prosperity and wealth. Its characteristic is such that any riches gained will eventually be lost. If found in the Self sector, whether male or female and no matter whether there are brilliant or auspicious stars around, is an indication for an unhappy childhood. This may have to do with one or more of the following: illnesses, poverty, loneliness, school-work problems or major personal disasters.

Void in the Self sector individuals very often have their own peculiar outlook on life. They don't say much and perplex people with their often changing personas. Behind their brooding façade is an active mind that wants to be recognized but at the same time, rejects contact. These people are creative and artistic. This dark star in the Self sector brings with it at least one major, heart-rending set-back.

The Void's contradictory streak comes to the fore if met up by Fire (C25) or Bell (C26) – either in the same sector, it's opposite or at 120°. This pairing-up ignites and initiates an explosive development which will have a tremendous up-lifting affect on one's life's work. Two evils definitely make up a good.

The Void works in conjunction with Punishment (below) – so read on.

C28. Punishment (地劫)

*T*he most powerful of the dark stars, this one wrecks destruction on this lifetime's two important areas: the prosperity self and the emotional self. The thing about these stars is they love to play games. They let you have, then they take away. In this instance, Punishment gives little, but takes away much. Is it then no surprise that the emotional self takes a beating too?

Ancient texts likens the Self sector with Punishment as "… A boat in a hurricane". Persons with Punishment in the Self sector will be small in stature, idiosyncratic and imaginative. They like to deal in financial matters. You will not find great orators among these individuals. In fact, many a times, they will find themselves tongue-tied or loath to speak up.

Both Punishment and Void bring great changes and destruction of the negative kind. Unlike the uprooting and turbulence of The General (A13) and The Pioneer (A14) which brings pioneering success, in the end all that Punishment and Void deliver are loss and despair.

It is imperative to remember NOT to start your own business with Punishment or Void in the Self, Karmic Wealth or Career sectors. This would include investing your own hard-earned money – any gains would be short-lived and the losses, great. A point about investing here: So long as you are not the business owner, for example, you are an investment manager employed to invest client money, Void or Punishment in these sectors will not affect your work.

Women with Punishment in the Self sector will be unhappy in love. However, with time, the detrimental effects of this star will weaken – you can find true love, albeit at a later stage in life.

Punishment or Void in the Self, Karmic Wealth or Career sectors would shine on professionals – doctors, lawyers, engineers where their quick, analytical mind and fine imagination can come to the fore.

The worst place one could find Punishment and Void would be on either side of the Self house. Any brilliant or auspicious stars in the Self would be dimmed considerably, leading to a life of much struggle and several ups and downs. In this case, study each of the 10-year periods life and look for your opportunities there indicated by the good stars. Those will be times when you can seize the moment and fly!

6 The Catalysts

That we are able to foretell exactly the happenings that will come to pass has, very simply, to do with the catalysts …

B y now, you will have familiarized yourself with the workings of Stargate. You may even have run your own birth chart and have gotten a few extraordinary insights into your life. It is here, in this chapter, that we deal with the crux of WHAT MAKES STARGATE UNIQUE. That we are able to foretell exactly the happenings that will come to pass has, very simply, to do with *the Catalysts.*

On the birth chart, out of the 14 major stars, four will carry 'attachments' or catalysts. These all-important indicators offer significant insight to the period under scrutiny. How fare the lifetime, each 10-year period or each specific year, can largely be determined by the appearance of the Catalysts and to what stars and chamber these are attached. The Catalysts are the pillars of your life. Together with the positions of the other major stars, whether auspicious or detriment, comes what is to be expected. On every birth chart constructed, look for these first. *The Catalysts determine what is.*

Chart Interpretation: *Look for the sets of four catalysts on each chart and discover their explanations on the following pages.*

The Wealth Catalyst ($)

The Wealth Catalyst attached to any major star carries the implication of income or gain. Specifically, this Catalyst brings in additional wealth or earthly possessions. From where the wealth comes depends on the star it is attached to and timing (which is shown on the chart).

The Power Catalyst (↗)

The Power Catalyst attached to a star indicates that that sector would be highly energized – given the go-ahead, so to speak. Relevant issues would be upheld with obstacles falling away.

The Fame Catalyst (✹)

Prominence shines in the House where Fame comes to rest or recognition for one's life's work. However, depending on surrounding stars, this could also mean unwanted attention is drawn in. A House with positive major stars indicates success and recognition gained through hard work – you've earned your wings. Watch out for the dark stars, however. Surrounded by these, Fame may usher in a bad press!

The Obstacle Catalyst (■)

This catalyst strikes a blow to the House or Stars it is attached to. A major lesson in one's life or any period it may find itself in. Unfortunately, expect to work extra hard and be prepared to be put to the test many a times. Look for a relief, for these are the times you will shine and be free of its clutches.

Heavenly Stem 1 - St1

A6. CRIMSON($)

Crimson (having to do with the emotions) with the Wealth Catalyst indicates emotional wealth – happiness. Blood or blood relations will bring wealth or will introduce propitious situations. This year, the sociable star smiles on you. So put yourself into the crowd – you have everything to gain!

A14. PIONEER(↗)

The Pioneer juggles different roles. With the Power Catalyst, we see a bigger role to play or a heavier burden in the House this star rests in. The Pioneer also stands for the introduction of new ways or concepts. The Power Catalyst here brings authority.

A4. COMMANDER(☼)

The Commander brings in wealth. With wealth in place, Fame follows.

A8. THE SUN(■)

The Sun stands for crowds, the majority or the general public. An obstructed Sun indicates generally being disapproved by the majority. However, there is another meaning if viewed from the other side: Success in "negative" roles. These would include for example, paramedics working among the sick or infirm; or, taking it further, actors in demonic parts – you get the idea! Under this curve of hazy light, you will shine.

The head, eyes and heart areas are all governed by The Sun. In eclipse, ailments with these areas will come to light. Be on the alert when this star enters the Health, or any of the "people" sectors, males especially.

Heavenly Stem 2 - St2

A2. INTELLIGENCE($)

The Strategist maneuvers and collects his due. However, if hemmed in by dark or obstructed stars, especially The Moon obstructed (■) on either side or opposite sectors, Intelligence ($) may spell certain misfortune – robbery, for instance. So be forewarned and you won't be taken by surprise.

A12. SCHOLAR(↗)

The Scholar stands for protection, solitude, litigation and injury. Power to the Scholar have the implication of adding weight to Scholar's traits. Negativity may be enhanced; take these in stride. They are, after all, not life threatening and look for redeeming qualities in the opposing houses or at 120°.

A1. EMPEROR(☼)

The Great One holds court and invites Fame in through his pioneering leadership. If hemmed in or opposed by dark stars, The Emperor with Fame, may gain popularity through misguided or fraudulent channels.

A8. THE MOON(■)

The Moon being a prosperous star and feminine, also stands for dimness and secrecy. Obstructions in these areas include economic loss, conspiracy or ruin, etc. brought on by a female.

Heavenly Stem 3 - St3

A5. WAIF($)

A lucky star, the Waif has to do with the emotions, enjoyment, sensitivity, gentleness and building great things from zero. The Wealth Catalyst uses (others') fortunes to build one's own fortunes e.g. finance and wealth management. Otherwise, the entertainment industry or anything having to do with enjoyment would work towards being wealth.

A2. INTELLIGENCE(↗)

Intelligence's abilities for strategic mobility, mechanics and agility would be enhanced by the Power catalyst. Recognize this individual by an impeccably kept desktop, office or home. Power gives him the reigns.

A17. LITERARY MINISTER(✿)

This individual will be basking in the spotlights in literary matters, education, the arts and major examinations. Note, however, any dark or inauspicious stars surrounding or opposing – the wrong or unwanted kind of publicity may be attracted around the above matters e.g. unearned credentials, manipulated test results, etc. all fall under this category as well!

A6. CRIMSON(■)

This unlucky catalyst, when attached to Crimson, obviously points to blood letting – serious accidents, operations, diseases of the blood. Crimson also guards the heart, the emotional self: A broken heart weeps in the Sector Crimson (?) chooses to enter.

Heavenly Stem 4 - St4

A8. THE MOON($)

The Moon has anything to do with females or quietude. The Wealth Catalyst brings in situations whereby fortunes can be gained by associations, businesses or trades dealing with feminine matters or partnerships with females. A quiet environment will also bring in success.

A5. THE WAIF(↗)

The Waif's abilities for building fortunes from nothing will be enhanced by the Power catalyst. Note any supportive stars around which will validate. However, if around inauspicious stars, The Waif(↗) would require great effort in regaining fortunes lost.

A2. INTELLIGENCE(✿)

Intelligence's penchant for strategy and action will be highlighted. You will see and hear a lot about this person. As his voice and personality comes to the fore, the opposition or obstructions retreat. Depending on the sector Intelligence with Fame(✳) falls into, the Self or the particular person in the sector clutches fame and action with his innovative ideas.

A10. THE MESSENGER(■)

Slander, litigation and suspicions will be enhanced with the Obstruction catalyst attached. There will also be undiscovered losses. If this star should come to rest in the Health sector, complicated and undiagnosed ailments may present themselves.

Heavenly Stem 5 - St5

A9. OPPORTUNITY($)

The star for socializing, partying and networking forms a fitting liaison with the Wealth catalyst and milks it for all it's worth. Look for opportunities in body-building, physical exercise or even the dance or hobby sectors. On these, the Wealth catalyst works its magic.

A8. THE MOON(↗)

This wealth star has its money management abilities boosted with the Power catalyst. These individuals will not fail to prosper with large sums of money under their supervision. Seriously consider a career in finance, equity and money management – everyone stands to gain under your auspices! And don't forget The Moon, being *yin*: You won't be turned down should you ask for help from your female supporters.

A3. THE SUN(☼)

Fame shines on those in the male, lighting or broadcasting industries. Note, however, The Sun, being bright and male, might not benefit from an extra mega-dose of the same. A burn out might result if one is not careful.

A2. INTELLIGENCE(■)

Strategic or mobility impediments. Obstructions to the thought process, movements etc. Well constructed ideas, alas, fall to seed. An obstructed Intelligence also brings out negative traits – the faint-hearted self. Otherwise, Intelligence becomes its own enemy. An over-bearing conviction of its own superior intelligence will work against the Self, inviting distrust all around.

Heavenly Stem 6 - St6

A4. COMMANDER($)

The Master Implementer will be handsomely rewarded. Throw him your plans and the reigns. This individual will carry them out to the hilt. Spectacular results inevitably brings in wealth for all. The Commander also comes with his own particular brand of a craft. Hone it to an art form – with Wealth behind, the rest will follow.

A9. OPPORTUNITY(↗)

This star of Socializing, Indulgence, Physical Exercise, Physique and Sports, also delves into the Occult. Power comes to him through the foregoing activities. Opportunity deals with indulgence in physical activities. However, with Power's helpful guidance, its wiser, hard-working, positive side would be brought to play. Opportunity at its most positive – a welcome to have in any sector.

A12. SCHOLAR(☼)

Fame attached to the Scholar's attributes of Protection and Elegance which culminates to eminence and distinction. You will be held in respect, even awe by many. This brilliant star lends an almost regal quality to the individual, without the crown and jewels.

A18. ARTS MINISTER(■)

The Arts Minister deals with the expressive Self and brings in slight speech impediments. With Obstruction blocking, watch out of verbal promises or agreements being refuted or denied. With this star combination, don't take any chances with (verbal) agreements. Commit anything of importance to the written form.

Heavenly Stem 7 - St7

A3. THE SUN($)

The most elegant of the stars, The Sun would be helped along by the Wealth Catalyst. The world recognizes its elegant ways and showers it with attention and lifting it to star status, so to speak. Thereon, the rewards surge in. Remember also, The Sun symbolizes the crowd, males and the media. From these channels wealth flows. The Sun($) in any sector during daylight hours makes its fortunes in full public view. After sunset, it is all veiled in secrecy.

A4. COMMANDER(↗)

A prosperous star in its own right, the Commander is our action hero. And with Power to boost, you can be sure to see him rewarded for his relentless efforts. Self-empowerment here is the key word. Delegate wisely; but never let go of the reigns. Because only you hold the power to your own destiny and ultimate success.

A7. THE VAULT(☼)

The Vault, possessing much wealth within its walls, deals with finance and financial matters. This individual has far to go with Fame attached. Many will hear of his wizardry in managing finance. On the reverse, albeit off-chance of things going awry, watch out for the detrimental stars. Their influence might make an infamous mockery of his name.

A5. THE WAIF(■)

Our lucky little star's outstanding quality is the ability to turn poverty to wealth. However, with Obstruction in tow, expect many wrong turns. At times, you may even contemplate giving up. Remember your key word: Persevere. You will get there in the end. The already emotional Waif will alas, have her heart broken. Just when it seemed she has grasped happiness, it turns to ashes and is scattered with the wind.

Heavenly Stem 8 - St8

A10. THE MESSENGER($)

In a sector that is also filled with several auspicious stars and few or none of the bad ones, The Messenger($) will bear the meaning of fortunes being made by the voice. However, any surrounding dark star will strip away any splendor and The Messenger with ($) attached will subsequently strike a loss through slander or litigation.

A3. THE SUN(↗)

The Sun with the Power catalyst carries the obvious trait of having the crowd, or male supporters on your side. Power to The Sun makes for a highly independent mind which gives rise to the pioneering spirit.

A18. ARTS MINISTER(☼)

An eloquent speaker, the Arts Minister is also a gifted engineer or scientist. Wherever he goes, Fame shines; for he speaks with sincerity and conviction.

A17. LITERARY MINISTER(■)

The written word is dealt a blow by Obstruction. Many a times, this carries the meaning of a lay-off or being fired. On the other hand, a documentation error will lead to great losses. Perhaps, also, the individual is weak in expressing himself in the written form. Be weary of recurring written errors.

Heavenly Stem 9 - St9

A12. SCHOLAR($)

A benevolent, protective star, The Scholar($) gives forth heirlooms or estate in money or a family business. This could also be a benevolent employer: the company one works for is especially generous in providing staff protection. Note this would only manifest itself in the presence of other beneficial stars in the same or opposite house.

A1. EMPEROR(↗)

Given Power's fiery headgear, the Emperor – already a hot headed individual – sees red. This is not one to bend, especially earlier on in life. It will take much effort from his ministers and advisors (the auspicious stars) to assist this individual to success, so let's hope they're around. If not – remember your catch phrase – She stoops to conquer.

A7. THE VAULT(✿)

The Vault, possessing much wealth within its walls, deals with finance and financial matters. Many will hear of his wizardry in managing finance. On the reverse, albeit off-chance of things going awry, watch out for the detrimental stars. Their influence might make an infamous mockery of his name.

A4. COMMANDER(■)

The Commander has his hands tied with Obstruction. If in business, this will manifest in cash flow problems, and if allowed to escalate – closure. Those in employment have the possibility of being terminated. Seek out the helpful brilliants. Never invest your own hard-earned cash, especially in your own business! The Commander also symbolizes sharp metal objects. Watch out for the Commander(■) coming to rest in the Health sector in any given year, which is a sign of injuries from metals, or operations.

Heavenly Stem 10 - St10

A14. PIONEER($)

The Pioneer, who destroys the old and starts afresh, is richly rewarded after spring-cleaning his house. With this star combination in any chamber, do not hesitate in pulling out all the weeds from your garden and throwing out everything that don't work. With your innovative ways and ideas, there is nothing to stop you attaining your goals and seize the ultimate prize.

A10. THE MESSENGER(↗)

Power to your communicative skills. Here we have a master communicator. So effective is she in delivering her pitch – you come away totally convinced and pleased with yourself for your wise decision. However, with dark stars opposing or inter-locking, The Messenger(↗) will mislead with slander. Ultimately, the karma she creates catches up.

A8. THE MOON(✳)

The Moon, a prosperity star, has also to do with females. Fame comes to you from money or financial matters and very likely this has to do with, or given a little push by your female sympathizers. The Moon is also mysterious and quiet. Fame takes on being well-known within a tight circle of friends.

A9. OPPORTUNITY(■)

Opportunity, has to do with socializing and hobbies (its furthest range being Indulgence). Opportunity gets into deep trouble when seized by the Obstruction catalyst. However, it is Stargate's peculiarity that Opportunity (■) always meets up with Pioneer ($) in its opposite chamber or at 120°. And here's salvation. Instead of heavy duty bad luck, we might see an increase in pointless socializing, followed by a bad hangover. Or there might be less or no socializing at all. Not altogether unwelcome, if only to keep us out of trouble.

7 The Obstruction Catalyst in the Houses

*The meaning of each
Obstruction Catalyst, as it
falls into each sector ...*

I n anticipation of the coming year (or any specific year, 10-year period, or the whole life), one of the ways of preparing for what lies ahead is to be told the bad news first. From this platform of the worst case scenario, we can then add on what remedy, if at all, is made available to us – where the auspicious stars are, where our power lies, how we are helped by any of the auspicious stars. The single most important element to look for would be The Obstruction Catalyst. When found in the Self sector, it wrecks havoc by various means, depending on the star it is attached to. You will find important clues as to what to expect as we go through each house and explain what Obstruction does to each of the major stars.

Obstruction (◼) in the Self House

A2. INTELLIGENCE(◼)

Any long-term plan, if launched in the time span that Obstruction prevails, will fall to seed. As we are also dealing with (lateral) movements here, watch out for losses as delays or destruction of deliveries, communication and travel plans, etc. become eminent. If allowed to play out its full force, the outcome would be feelings of despair and being out of control.

A3. THE SUN(◼)

An Obstructed Sun in the Self Chamber. Watch out for injuries or ailments to the head area, especially the eyes; also the heart. If you are normally insightful or intuitive, be aware of this power being dimmed or obstructed during the period. The Sun also stands for one's reputation – your good name may be at stake. Be weary of partnerships, especially with males. Avoid these if at all possible. By the same token, females would be more sympathetic to you at this time.

A4. COMMANDER(◼)

The Commander, being a prosperity star, when in retrograde deals out sudden additional management expenses. Your carefully worked out financial plans abruptly gets replaced from circumstances beyond your control. Great challenges lie in trying to make ends meet. On another front, metals cross you: anticipate accidents with knives and other sharp objects. Inherently, a severing of a relationship. Hence, an operation is not out of your agenda, metaphorically or otherwise.

A5. THE WAIF(■)

A knife pierces through the emotional Self. Surround yourself with tender loving care – for if you don't, no one will. A period of feeling unloved and neglected, low self-esteem and yes, brace for a ride on your emotional roller-coaster. Would it help if we suggested most of this suffering is self-inflicted? When this star for enjoyment is in retrograde, watch out for disasters at play, literally. For it is at times of fun that you will suddenly find yourself face to face with trouble. Avoid the 'fun' places if at all possible during this time.

A6. CRIMSON (■)

Crimson, having to do with emotional matters and blood or blood relations. By nature, this star keeps things to himself. Are you hurting but putting on a brave smile for the world? Nurture yourself at this time. Blood or blood related diseases or blood brothers causing the distress in the heart or head. So watch out for the related outcome – litigations.

A8. THE MOON(■)

The Moon, which favors income or prosperity, is in retrograde. Do not be involved with investments (other than managing other people's money) at this time. Veiled in quietude and secrecy which is one of The Moon's many faces, go over unanswered questions, or events which bother but which you cannot put a finger to. In these may hide an as yet unnoticed time-bomb. Litigation will be high on your agenda for this period. Avoid business associations with females, who may be the perpetrators of the bad news.

A9. OPPORTUNITY(■)

This star of entertainment and socializing turns dark with Obstruction attached. At its darkest, physical activities and hobbies turn into indulgence and obsessions. Vice dens are not out of the question. Need we go on? The depths of despair are unfathomable. An item or person you hold close will be ripped from you.

A10. THE MESSENGER(■)

The unfortunate associations with The Messenger in retrograde come to the fore with slander, law suits, disagreements or even a slip of the tongue which lands the Self in hot water. Pay special attention to private affairs – as the Obstruction Catalyst go against these. Activities involving publicizing the Self should be avoided; as, with Obstruction in tow, only the negative results will emerge.

A17. LITERARY MINISTER(■)

The written word carries with it untold misery for the Self. Go over any legal documents or papers of importance meticulously during this period. Assert great care in any self-written articles or documents for public view. Your problems start with contractual matters.

A18. ARTS MINISTER (■)

A price to be paid for errors made during speech or the written word. Double-checking notes or documents may alleviate the harm. Endless delays in contractual matters, with much arguments and complaints in between, are the call for the day.

Obstruction (■) in the Elders House

The Elders House deals with those above us – our parents, bosses and, if in business, clients. The Obstruction catalyst in this chambers brings problems associated with these people.

A2. INTELLIGENCE(■)

Plans are being drawn up against the Elders.

A3. THE SUN(■)

Unfavourable forces are acting against those above you. Be weary of frauds and cheats surrounding these people, males especially.

A4. COMMANDER(■)

The hot-tempered Commander in retrograde here indicates a break-up of a client/parent relationship. On the other hand, the boss may take an overly hard-line stance. Beware!

A5. THE WAIF(■)

The boss or client may be giving you a hard time. With the emotionally unstable Waif in retrograde attached to these people, who could blame?

A6. CRIMSON (■)

An emotional set back for those in the Elders Chamber. Also, a falling out with close relations.

A8. THE MOON(■)

Underhanded, almost undetected mischief is in the air, directed at those above you. A woman is behind the scene. A major prosperity star in retrograde means finances turn for the worse.

A9. OPPORTUNITY(■)

A newly acquired vice or obsession may cause a severe blow to those in the Elders house.

A10. THE MESSENGER(■)

Too much has been said involving people in the Elders sector. Events may turn litigious.

A17. LITERARY MINISTER(■)

A breach of contract, errors or oversight. And the Elders are called in to deal with this.

A18. ARTS MINISTER (■)

The Elders have to deal with matters concerning a breach of contract.

Obstruction (■)
in the Karmic Wealth House

The Karmic Wealth Chamber deals with our emotional well-being. With the Obstruction Catalyst in residence, expect very few moments of peaceful contemplation! Here, the emotional Self takes a beating.

A2. INTELLIGENCE(■)

The ghost of a failed plan comes back to haunt. The Self cannot let go of having been cheated. Blaming of the self is also the cause of many a sleepless night.

A3. THE SUN(■)

Emotional fatigue causes the male Self to suffer a misfortune due to fraud, or his own oversight. If the Self is female, this occurs to the man in her life.

A4. COMMANDER(■)

The Commander in retrograde here takes a hard-line and you decide to sever an important relationship. However, the hard-hearted does not escape the hurt.

A5. THE WAIF(■)

This star which rules emotional well-being, enters the chamber of the emotions. Unfortunately, in retrograde, The Waif here deals with deep sorrow.

A6. CRIMSON (■)

Mistrust and a severing of close relationships due to a dispute over family/shareholder money, legacies, etc.

A8. THE MOON(■)

Emotional fatigue or instability causes the female Self the loss of a small fortune. A vicious cycle may form as she vexes over the loss and so, becomes depressive. If the Self is a male, the problem applies to the Spouse.

A9. OPPORTUNITY(■)

Opportunity in retrograde in the chamber of emotions has his love wrenched from him by another.

A10. THE MESSENGER(■)

A falling-out with that special someone, litigation, dispute – any situation in which you might have said too much – causes the regret. Just don't let it hang over you for too long!

A17. LITERARY MINISTER(■)

An oversight or forgetfulness leads to documentation errors. Much regret and self-reproaching ensues.

A18. ARTS MINISTER (■)

A deep sense of remorse over mistakes in documents or an event which was overlooked.

Obstruction (■) *in the Properties/Business House*

An important Chamber to check your fortunes – for herein lie your home, any real estate you may own and the seat of your business. The Obstruction attachment here may have major cataclysmic consequences. Need we emphasize that any major movements or plans should be shelved – for the time being at least? At this point, check that your Life Chart does not have the Obstruction catalyst in the Properties sector. This star placement ensures your downfall in business. Likewise, investments bought with your own hard-earned savings will be reduced to nil.

A2. INTELLIGENCE(■)

A serious, consequential change occurring in the home or business, leading to much unhappiness and discord.

A3. THE SUN(■)

Misfortune befalling the male member(s) of the family. Otherwise, a depreciation of assets due to fraud or misrepresentations.

A4. COMMANDER(■)

This prosperity star when joined with Obstruction, takes away a major chunk of the family's regular income. Fortunes suddenly take a turn for the worse.

A5. THE WAIF(■)

Misfortunes befalling the younger members of the family or business. Otherwise, a fortune painstakingly built will be lost.

A6. CRIMSON (■)

Mistrust and a severing of close relationships due to a dispute over family/shareholder money, legacies, etc.

A8. THE MOON(■)

Misfortunes befalling the female member(s) of the family/ business; the slow but sure siphoning away of family/shareholder fortunes, theft, etc. A quiet loss under the cover of stillness and darkness.

A9. OPPORTUNITY(■)

This menacing star combination turns its attention to the minors here. Watch out for injuries to small children in the home. On the other hand, Opportunity made retrograde by Obstruction, pushes vices or obsessions towards minors.

A10. THE MESSENGER(■)

Much disagreement circulating in the home/business. If allowed to escalate into serious discord – the scene for litigation would have been set. There is an indication of incarceration.

A17. LITERARY MINISTER(■)

The Obstruction catalyst, when joined with the Literary Minister, brings a funeral to the home. Assets or properties documentation errors will also be discovered and have to be set right.

A18. ARTS MINISTER (■)

This star made retrograde by the Obstruction catalyst carries strong indications of a funeral occurring in the home. At the same time, you will be asked to deal with asset problems.

Obstruction (■) in the Career House

Are you noticing that nothing seems to go smoothly at the workplace – be it staff relationship or workflow hiccups, work-related sicknesses, etc.? Check that the Obstruction Catalyst is not in this sector of your life. Otherwise, you now know why ...

A2. INTELLIGENCE(■)

A planning or implementation error that had gone unnoticed for a long time, suddenly comes to the fore, resulting in loss. This can also take the form of an erroneous job change.

A3. THE SUN(■)

A colleague has pulled the carpet from under your feet, resulting in your loss of face or trust or both! Read up on how to deal with the office bully – and It's probably a He.

A4. COMMANDER(■)

Albeit a prosperity star, the Obstructed Commander here represents disputes over money at the workplace or, that a loss occurs because of money. Also, the star element of metal crosses you. Beware of injuries from metals, operations, etc. Personality clashes result in loss.

A5. THE WAIF(■)

A serious accident or workplace disaster is waiting to happen. Otherwise, negativity hangs heavily in the air.

A6. CRIMSON (■)

The Self is called upon or finds herself having to deal with underhanded behavior at the workplace. Alternatively, an office romance leaves you in the dust. Be weary of being swept away!

A8. THE MOON(■)

Your problems come from disputes regarding money – commission, shares, etc., and a female colleague will be behind it all.

A9. OPPORTUNITY(■)

The star for networking, unfortunately works against you with the Obstruction catalyst attached. You fall through the net.

A10. THE MESSENGER(■)

The workplace is rife with idle talk. Whether having anything to do with it or not, the Self is inextricably drawn into its web. Litigious in nature, a loss will have to be borne.

A17. LITERARY MINISTER(■)

Serious errors within documents resulting in a reprimand. This star, having to do with examinations, with the Obstruction catalyst in tow, has the meaning of a fall from grace – you fail the test. You face the danger of being let go.

A18. ARTS MINISTER (■)

There are as yet unnoticed errors in important documents that will manifest themselves in problems and loss. Check the written word carefully and speak with clarity – for therein may contain the seed of your downfall.

Obstruction (■) in the Staff House

The Obstruction Catalyst here suggests your staff getting the upper hand and the Self may be called upon to deal with disgruntled workers or industrial action. Injuries, workmen compensation, claims from staff, etc. all come to the fore with the arrival of this menacing guest.

A2. INTELLIGENCE(■)

Workers and staff have a plot up their sleeves. On the other hand, a staff's blueprint or plans contain an error which results in your loss.

A3. THE SUN(■)

Be weary of male employees trying to get the upper hand. Deception or fraud may be at play. Staff mishap or oversight results in a dent to the firm's reputation. Guard against workmen injuries occurring to the head, chest or eye areas.

A4. COMMANDER(■)

Albeit a prosperity star, the Obstructed Commander here takes on the meaning of disputes over money at work.

A5. THE WAIF(■)

Emotional entanglements with a staff or staff members resulting in much chagrin. Remember this: With the Obstruction in tow, office romances never pay off.

A6. CRIMSON (■)

A relationship with a staff member is emotionally charged and detrimental to the Self. Alternatively, a serious physical injury with much blood loss. Staff being secretive and enigmatic? It has all to do with the Obstruction catalyst's decision to visit.

A8. THE MOON(■)

Money entices and a major staff defection may be occurring stealthily right under the nose. Be aware of females.

A9. OPPORTUNITY(■)

Staff members may be discovered to have taken on a vice. Also, be weary of a pilfering of top staff by the competition.

A10. THE MESSENGER(■)

A letting go of steam of the verbal nature with staff members. Brace for an escalation to litigious levels. Verbal dissatisfaction abounds. Or, staff members' constant slips of the tongue land them in hot water.

A17. LITERARY MINISTER(■)

The written word or errors within it bring many problems. Staff members going against the office code of practice.

A18. ARTS MINISTER (■)

Contractual problems arising with staff members; a breaking away from an agreed code of conduct by staff. Much time and resource will be spent.

Obstruction (■) *in the Travel/Migration House*

The Travel/Migration Sector, having to do with overseas connections, particularly immigration or a change of background as in a job change. The Obstruction Catalyst in here brings certain misfortunes following the change. This is not a time to start ventures with overseas contacts.

A2. INTELLIGENCE(■)

An entrapment awaits you at the other side of the horizon. On the other hand, go back to the drawing board –something is amiss with preliminary plans. Or mishaps with travel or delivery plans.

A3. THE SUN(■)

Two scenarios: You meet up with frauds from another land or you deal with fraudulent matters/people after a change of background, putting your reputation on the spot. Be aware of males.

A4. COMMANDER(■)

Fortunes lost from dealings with foreign contacts. Alternatively, after a major change of background e.g. a job change or migration, the Self sustains injuries from metals or sharp objects – an operation perhaps.

A5. THE WAIF(■)

Just as you let your guard down during enjoyment or fun time is how the Obstruction Catalyst attached to the Waif catches you unawares.

A6. CRIMSON (■)

After a change of background, the Self encounters a serious injury (blood loss). On the other hand, a broken romance in another land. Be weary of underhanded dealings with foreigners; someone is trying to pull the carpet from under your feet.

A8. THE MOON(■)

The Moon deals with prosperity; and so, a loss occurring because of or after a change of background. Be weary of females.

A9. OPPORTUNITY(■)

Much aggravation regarding dealings with people of a foreign land or after migration or a change of job. This has a direct adverse affect on your career or business. Be weary of night spots, clubs and other social establishment. Opportunity with the Obstruction catalyst has a way of ensnaring you at these places.

A10. THE MESSENGER(■)

After a change of background, you will find yourself dealing with litigious matters. A slip of the tongue may land you in hot water!

A17. LITERARY MINISTER(■)

Problems arising after migrating to another country or a change in employment. This dark catalyst bodes ill for job interviews or any testing of your abilities. Be on the lookout for document errors, especially with regard to figures.

A18. ARTS MINISTER (■)

Problems arising after migrating to another country or a change in employment. The Self encounters disputes regarding contractual details or fraudulent contracts. Be on the lookout for document errors, especially with regard to figures.

Obstruction (■) in the Health Sector

Your health comes under attack during the period that the Obstruction Catalyst invites itself into the Health Chamber. The various ills (which may not confine only to health issues) are defined by the star attachment.

A2. INTELLIGENCE(■)

The nervous system, liver or bile.

A3. THE SUN(■)

Illnesses having to do with the head, heart or eyes.

A4. COMMANDER(■)

Infections of the lungs or breathing problems. The Commander also stands for metals – an indication of knife injuries; or operations.

A5. THE WAIF(■)

Problems with the kidneys, reproductive or sexual organs.

A6. CRIMSON (■)

All blood related diseases, the heart, gynecological disorders or allergies.

A8. THE MOON(■)

The eyes, nervous and lymphatic systems.

A9. OPPORTUNITY(■)

Ailments with the reproductive organs, kidneys, abdominal, up to the liver area.

A10. THE MESSENGER(■)

Infections of the mouth or tongue areas.

A17. LITERARY MINISTER(■)

Illnesses of the skin surface.

A18. ARTS MINISTER (■)

Illnesses of the skin surface.

Obstruction (■) in the Prosperity House

The Prosperity Chamber in jeopardy takes on the meaning of fortunes lost, or disputes and misfortune arising because of money.

A2. INTELLIGENCE(■)

Ideas or implementation problems which result in loss. Do you have a faint heart when it comes to dealing with finances? Are your stocks sending you on a roller coaster ride? Look before you leap. You are looking at wrong decisions leading to financial loss.

A3. THE SUN(■)

A betrayal undermines you – resulting in loss. Otherwise, because of money or money invested, a serious blow to the reputation. Be aware of males.

A4. COMMANDER(■)

The Commander, if joined by the Obstruction Catalyst, means only one thing – your Prosperity Self takes a beating. During this period, you will have a hard time trying to balance your accounts.

A5. THE WAIF(■)

Conflicts arising from problems having to do with money or gain. The emotional Self takes a beating.

A6. CRIMSON (■)

Crimson(■) in the Prosperity Chamber points to conflicts arising from monetary disputes and/or those nearest and dearest (your blood relations, that is) getting grazed for which you are called to spend on.

A8. THE MOON(■)

The Moon, having to do with income or prosperity, is in retrograde. Those under you (especially the females) suffer losses which may come from investments or speculations. The implication of having been lured into bogus investments is also present.

A9. OPPORTUNITY(■)

Are you overly indulgent on yourself and spending way above limits on an expensive hobby?

A10. THE MESSENGER(■)

Litigious matters which throws your budget completely off. Conversely, money brings problems of a litigious nature.

A17. LITERARY MINISTER(■)

The written word goes awry and you will find that contractual errors or oversight lead to loss. Burn the mid-night oil if you have to, but check twice through all the fine print.

A18. ARTS MINISTER (■)

The Self encounters betrayal or loss from contractual disasters. Go through all fine print once again or employ professionals to do that for you – you'll thank your lucky stars for having done that.

Obstruction (▪) in the Minors House

This Chamber deals with those under you – most notably children and principal employees. The Obstruction in the Minors Sector indicates unfortunate happenings with these people, or that these individuals bring problems.

A2. INTELLIGENCE(▪)

Children or senior employees are formulating a plan to undermine the Self. Otherwise, if those under you are putting together a strategy or plan, a serious flaw gets included.

A3. THE SUN(▪)

An Obstructed Sun in the Minors Chamber stands for those under the Self being betrayed; or the Self is betrayed by these individuals, especially if these are male.

A4. COMMANDER(▪)

The Commander, if joined by the Obstruction Catalyst, means only one thing – your prosperity Self takes a beating. In the Minors sector, it takes on the added misfortune of seriously harming the relationship.

A5. THE WAIF(▪)

The Self's relationship with his children or principal employees undergoes a shift or a great test.

A6. CRIMSON (■)

Be aware of emotional distress among children or senior employees. These people may also be the cause of your unrest. Be weary of unreasonable, cowardly behavior.

A8. THE MOON(■)

The Moon, having to do with income or prosperity, is in retrograde. Those under you (especially the females) suffer losses which may come from investments or speculations. The implication of having been lured into bogus investments is also present.

A9. OPPORTUNITY(■)

Opportunity(■) in the Minors Chamber indicates those under you may be involved in a love triangle. Unless other supportive stars prevail, these persons will be left.

A10. THE MESSENGER(■)

The Messenger in retrograde in the Minors Chamber tells of litigious or libelous matters surround those under you.

A17. LITERARY MINISTER(■)

The written word is broken by the children or senior employees – a broken pledge involving your minors. Or, on the other hand, a serious error by these individuals results in your loss.

A18. ARTS MINISTER (■)

The Self encounters theft or is betrayed by those under him. This has mainly to do with the written word, in either documents or contractual form. Someone may also be going back on his word.

Obstruction (■) in the Spouse Sector

The Spouse Chamber deals with your spouse or the person with whom you are sharing an intimate relationship with. The Obstruction Catalyst(■) in the Spouse Sector therefore talks about destructive influences brought on by the spouse, or that which will be experienced by the spouse. Check with your Self Sector for detrimental stars to ascertain that you are not the cause for your spouse's ills.

A2. INTELLIGENCE(■)

Strategies and plans go awry for the spouse. There will also be travel-related problems to be dealt with.

A3. THE SUN(■)

An Obstructed Sun in the Spouse Sector stands for betrayal, lies or untruths that has to do with the spouse, the spouse is lied to or an erroneous decision by the spouse which leads to loss.

A4. COMMANDER(■)

The Commander, being a prosperity star, when entangled with the Obstruction Catalyst, spells out losses for the spouse. Be aware of injuries from metals, etc; otherwise an omen for an operation.

A5. THE WAIF(■)

The spouse goes through an emotionally upsetting time which may be brought on by a tremendous failure or loss.

A6. CRIMSON (■)

Your spouse undergoes emotional distress. Crimson, also having close associations with blood, in retrograde also spells out a serious accident or injury for the spouse.

A8. THE MOON(■)

The Moon, which favors income or prosperity, is in retrograde. The spouse experiences a loss in monetary terms. There may also be an enticement that leads to loss, having to do with the Self or spouse.

A9. OPPORTUNITY(■)

This star of entertainment and socializing turns retrograde and shows its ugly side. With the Obstruction catalyst attached in the Spouse sector there is strong indication of a taking on of some form of vice by the spouse. Disappoints prevail, arising from unexpected sources.

A10. THE MESSENGER(■)

The Messenger in retrograde in the Spouse Chamber tells of litigious matters for the spouse to deal with. On the other hand – a quarrelsome spouse.

A17. LITERARY MINISTER(■)

The written word brings in turbulence for the spouse. These will be in the form of services of writs, friends being laid off, divorce, deaths, etc.

A18. ARTS MINISTER (■)

The Spouse encounters theft or is betrayed. On the other hand, she may receive unfortunate news in the form of writs or notices of friends being laid off, divorces, deaths, etc.

Obstruction (■) in the Peers Chamber

The Peers Chamber deals with your peers – brothers and sisters, partners, same ranking colleagues, friends, classmates, and last but not least, your rivals. The Obstruction catalyst in the Peers Chamber, therefore, deals with problems brought on by these people.

A2. INTELLIGENCE(■)

Long-term plans with your peers fall part. Or, you are plotted against by your partners and associates.

A3. THE SUN(■)

An Obstructed Sun in the Peers Chamber stands for betrayal by male siblings, partners, close friends, colleagues, etc.

A4. COMMANDER(■)

The Commander, being a prosperity star, when in retrograde in the Peers Sector, deals with a falling out or break-up over money with partners or siblings.

A5. THE WAIF(■)

Siblings, partners etc. come face to face with trouble just as they are having a good time. Avoid the 'fun' places if at all possible during this time. An emotionally upsetting time for these people, which may have to do with a small fortune being made and lost.

A6. CRIMSON (■)

Your peers are the cause of your emotional distress. Note Crimson with the Obstruction catalyst in the Peers Sector is clear indication of events or projects falling apart. It is best to go it alone in this instance.

A8. THE MOON(■)

The Moon, which favors income or prosperity, is in retrograde in the Peers Chamber. The image of enticement which lays the trap for downfall. Do not fall for any get rich quick scheme or other similar snare. Income or property will be in jeopardy, especially if these involve exclusivity or secrecy. Most likely, females will be the temptress.

A9. OPPORTUNITY(■)

This star of entertainment and socializing, with the Obstruction catalyst attached in Peers sector symbolizes obsessions in vice establishments with close associates. As this strongly implicates a non-constructive, harmful relationship, it is best to sever any ties and go it alone, until such time that favors a mutually complimentary relationship.

A10. THE MESSENGER(■)

The Messenger in retrograde in the Peers Chamber has to do with libel or slanders, law suits, and disagreements with your peers.

A17. LITERARY MINISTER(■)

The written word is torn up in the Peers Sector. A contractual dispute leading to a break-up with partners or siblings.

A18. ARTS MINISTER (■)

Peers plot against you with documentation or any other form of the written word.

8 *The Milestones* *4 stars*

These stars will lead you to your chart with their accurately predicted milestones.

*T*he Milestones in the various years of one life are indicative of major events - one's marriage (or an important, karmic relationship), the arrival of children or major catalytic events such as deaths. These are life's turning points, heralded by the following important stars.

A NOTE ON CHARTING

It is Stargate's inherent quality to be accurate to the finest details of the life – provided that the birth hour is accurate. Based on the (known) birth hour, if a chart appears to be "off", that birth chart is probably not yours. Consult the charts for hours before or after your claimed birth hour. The positions of the major stars and the milestones will indicate whether you have found your Stargate. When you are comfortable with major past events and people, you will have found your own Stargate. With these events in place, you can proceed to view the future with confidence.

C29. *The Lover* (紅鸞)

T his enchanted star forms a pair with Happiness (C30) at its opposite house; i.e. if, for example, the Lover is found in the Self House, for sure Happiness would be in the Travel Sector, its opposite. The Lover signifies betrothal, whilst Happiness brings its crystallization – a newborn. Because these two stars are so closely interrelated, and stars in opposing houses always relate to each other, the betrothal/newborn factors can be cross-referenced with surrounding stars. The Lover and its surrounding stars can relate to the unborn child; and Happiness and its sisters can point to events surrounding the lovers.

The Lover does well with the Literary Minister (B17) or the Arts Minister (B18) at 120° both sides (beginning with where the Lover is as the first house, count to the fourth house) – as being most auspiciously placed conducive to a happy relationship. For those who are unattached, this star combination brings an engagement, betrothal or the beginning of a new, committed relationship.

This star of betrothal, however, forms an uneasy alliance if met up by her flirtatious friends e.g. (A6) Crimson and (A9) Opportunity. Watch out for a clandestine affair in the brewing.

In old-age, the appearance of The Lover in any sector becomes the presage to serious illness.

C30. *Happiness* (天喜)

A baby is along the way should this bright little star fall into the Minors or Properties Sectors. Still unsure? Whether it is a wanted pregnancy or not – check for other auspicious or bright stars surrounding – another clear sign. And prepare for a baby shower nine months later!

Happiness, being closely associated with The Lover, the marriage or relationship star, can also be used to gauge the state of a romance at any given period or year. Happiness, if surrounded by dark or inauspicious stars, tells of an imminent break-up however much the Self wants the affair to work.

Also, the Lover/Happiness double-stars together form a prosperity duo for the Self. However, they need the Power catalyst or Completion (B22) at the same House, its opposite, or at 120° (count to the fourth house left or right from where Lover or Happiness is).

C31. *Opposition* (天刑)

*N*eed we spell out the implications of this fearful star? Unfortunately, if found in any relationship chambers e.g. The Elders, Peers, Minors, Spouse or Staff, it spells certain disasters especially if supported by the dark, inauspicious or any star in retrograde. A strong indication of death from serious illness or sudden catastrophic events.

However, if the same or opposite house does not contain any of the dark or inauspicious stars, all this star would be concerned with are disciplinary matters. We would be dealing with Self-discipline or Self-punishment. On the other hand, the tri-star formation of Opposition, The Sun (A3) and the Scholar (A12), whether in the same or the opposite Chamber or at 120°, indicates an individual who will follow a career in law. Or, after a catalytic event, the Self sees a whole new horizon opening and goes forth to attain outstanding success.

If teamed with the flirtatious stars Crimson (A6) and Opportunity (A9) in the same or the opposite Chamber or at 120°, Finality has a grounding effect on these flighty individuals. The Self then easily eschews the characteristics of the Tease. With self-discipline installed, the go-getting qualities of Crimson and Opportunity come to the fore. We would be seeing a self-disciplined, hard-working and focused individual. Under these circumstances, albeit its name, Opposition becomes a welcome, positive influence.

C32. *Encounter* (天姚)

*A*n accidental encounter that sends the heart aflutter? The sudden arrival of a stranger who becomes the turning point in your once ordinary existence? We all know that feeling; and when these happen, chances are Encounter has woven its gossamer fingers over your eyes and around your heart. As it comes to rest in the Marriage Chamber, expect an affair that is brought about by a magical, mystical encounter – the stuff that romance novels are made of. If teamed by the Literary and Arts Ministers (B17 & 18), the heart defies gravity and no amount of cajole, flatter or threat could pull you back to earth!

Encounter aided by surrounding bright or auspicious stars and catalysts (in the same or opposite chamber or at 120°), and in the Self, Career or Prosperity Sectors, this star of romance becomes an indicator of wealth brought in by the opposite sex. In this instance, don't hesitate in following a career in support of the opposite sex – for you will be generously rewarded. Encounter, at its finest, takes on the qualities of prosperity.

However, at its core, Encounter deals out clandestine affairs, sprinkling chance encounters and frivolous romantic pursuits along her path. Faced with dark catalysts or stars in retrograde, Encounter turns sour. A chance encounter turns into an obsession – opening the Self to certain disaster and downfall.

$\mathscr{9}$ *Chart Interpretation*

A house where you can find success would have more positive stars outshining the bad ones.

Whether a house works for the people or thing it represents is entirely dependant upon the influence of the stars within it at any given time. A house can contain up to two major stars with or without the catalysts attached, plus six others which can be any of the Auspicious or Inauspicious stars. A house where you can find success would have more positive stars outshining the bad ones. Stars in the opposite house also play an influential role.

The Auspicious stars come in three pairs – The Left and Right Ministers (B15 & B16), The Literary and the Arts Ministers (B17 & B18), and Stardust and Delight (B19 & B20). These should be properly paired up in the same or opposite chambers. Without the other's support, a lone Auspicious Star would have its powers dimmed and might be made even weaker if Dark Stars surround.

what about Winged Horse (B21) and Completion B22 no need to be paired up?

The Dark Stars are six: C23 – The Ram, C24 Spinning Top, C25 Fire, C26 Bell and C27 The Void. A chamber would be cast in darkness should it contain more Dark Stars than Auspicious. It is well to remember that, whether Auspicious or Dark stars, we have them all spread throughout our chart; and as we move through each period of our lives, different sectors, in turn, will come to the fore and shine while others will be thrown into darkness. A good harvest does not last forever; nor can disaster trail you without end. This is the lesson that the stars and the universe teach us.

July 1, 1961   6 PM   (6:45 PM to be more exact)

PROSPERITY 2046-2055 / 86-95	MINORS 2056-2065 / 96-105	SPOUSE 2066-2075 / 106-115	PEERS 2076-2085 / 116-125
o A8 Moon C32 Encounter	△ A9 Opportunity B16 Right Minister B19 Stardust	o A5 Waif o A10 Messenger $ C B26 Bell	o A4 Commander o A11 Mirror B15 Left Minister C B24 Spinning Top C B28 Punishment C30 Happiness
St10/Br6 Snake 9-11am	St1/Br7 Horse 11am-1pm	St2/Br8 Goat 1-3pm	St3/Br9 Monkey 3-5pm

HEALTH 2036-2045 / 76-85	THE SELF 1966-1975 / 6-15
o A7 Vault △ A6 Crimson	o A3 Sun 🏹 △ A12 Scholar B22 Completion
St9/Br5 Dragon 7-9am	St4/Br10 Rooster 5-7pm

THE EMPEROR'S STARGATE
ON YOUR LIFE

This Chart is for	: Diana
You are a	: Yin Female
Chinese Birth Year	: St8Br2
Chinese Birth Month	: Lunar Month 5
Chinese Birth Date	: 19th
You are born between	: 5-7pm
Your animal sign is	: The Ox

Color Code	The Catalysts	Star Brightness
Red - Year under review	$ Prosperity	● Brilliant
Blue - The 10-Year Chart	✿ Fame	o Bright
Black - The Life Chart	🏹 Power	△ Twinkling
	■ Obstruction	× Dark

TRAVEL 2026-2035 / 66-75	ELDERS 1976-1985 / 16-25
	o A13 General C B23 Ram
St8/Br4 Rabbit 5-7am	St5/Br11 Dog 7-9pm

STAFF 2016-2025 / 56-65	CAREER 2006-2015 / 46-55	PROPERTIES 1996-2005 / 36-45	KARMIC 1986-1995 / 26-35
o A14 Pioneer B20 Delight C B27 Void C29 The Lover	B18 Arts Minister ✿ B17 Literary Minister ■ C31 Opposition	o A1 Emperor B25 Fire	△ A2 Intelligence B21 Winged Horse
St7/Br3 Tiger 3-5am	St8/Br2 Ox 1-3am	St7/Br1 Rat 11pm-1am	St6/Br12 Pig 9-11pm

A princess's chart

*D*iana Spencer was transformed over night from a shy kindergarten teacher to an icon. Destined to become the most photographed woman who ever lived, her amazing lifetime was daunted only by her sudden and tragic death. We shall trace her life's path through Stargate, in retrospect.

The Self

A3 THE SUN (↗)   Yang with the Power catalyst carries the trait of having the crowd, or male supporters on Diana's side. Power to Yang gave her a highly independent mind and gave rise to her pioneering spirit. Under the Sun's influence, she was a careful individual who was also prone to extravagance.

A12 THE SCHOLAR   The Star of Protection, points to her family's earldom; taking this further – her marriage into royalty.

B22 COMPLETION   Completion in the Self sector makes for an upright honest individual with a big heart. This star indicates a rewarding lifetime of wealth and prosperity without the rigmaroles of toils, hardships or great changes. On-going wealth was in her Self House.

Elders

A13 THE GENERAL   Angry, hot-tempered parents. When found in one of the relationship houses, this star stands for aloofness and separation and Diana's cool relationship with her parents.

B23 THE RAM   A dark, attacking star. Together with the General in this house, we see the marriage break-up of her parents. The Ram also has detrimental influences on the opposite stars.

Opposing the Elders House

These are not explained or listed under the Major Stars

A7 THE VAULT   The Ram gives forth toils and hardships to the *Not listed on P. 63* family home.

A6 CRIMSON   With the Ram's influence, a hurtful blood relationship, from the female side.

section, which only lists influences on the houses they reside in, not on the houses they oppose

Karmic Wealth

A2 INTELLIGENCE   The Self is preoccupied with heavy thoughts.

B21 THE WINGED HORSE   An busy individual who is afraid to stop. Teamed with Intelligence, the indication is for an exhausting road ahead for an extremely clever and agile individual. Hemmed in by the dark stars Ram and Fire, the Winged Horse will encounter accidents or danger whilst on the road.

Opposing the Karmic Health House

A8 THE MOON   At the opposing chamber, the Moon also influenced her psyche. Diana spent much time in solitude contemplation – a deep, wise individual with a colorful imagination.

C32 ENCOUNTER   This star of romantic encounters opposite the Karmic Wealth, with the Moon accompanying point to a secret alliance – unhappy thoughts resulting from secretive encounters.

Properties

A1 THE EMPEROR   The Emperor – divinatory meaning is 'of the head' or 'the highest order'. While this may point to the rest of us living "on high grounds or the higher floors of an apartment", it is indicative of Diana living in palatial surroundings.

B25 FIRE   Although a dark star, Fire is grouped in the same chamber with The Emperor and opposing are (A9) Opportunity and (B16) The Right Minister and (B19) Stardust. This represents a star grouping of the highest order. In this sector of business venture – Diana had brilliantly carved out her own life's work.

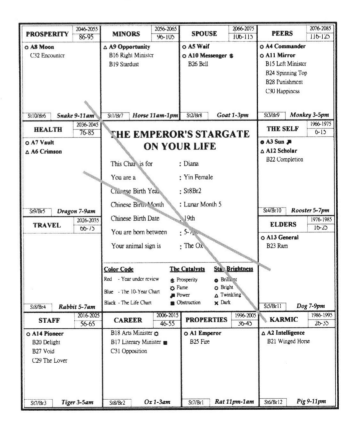

PROSPERITY	2046-2055 86-95	MINORS	2056-2065 96-105	SPOUSE	2066-2075 106-115	PEERS	2076-2085 116-125
o A8 Moon C32 Encounter		△ A9 Opportunity B16 Right Minister B19 Stardust		o A5 Waif o A10 Messenger $ B26 Bell		o A4 Commander o A11 Mirror B15 Left Minister B24 Spinning Top B28 Punishment C30 Happiness	
St10/Br6 *Snake 9-11am*		St1/Br7 *Horse 11am-1pm*		St2/Br8 *Goat 1-3pm*		St3/Br9 *Monkey 3-5pm*	

HEALTH 2036-2045 76-85 — o A7 Vault, △ A6 Crimson — St9/Br5 *Dragon 7-9am*

THE EMPEROR'S STARGATE ON YOUR LIFE

This Chart is for : Diana
You are a : Yin Female
Chinese Birth Year : St8Br2
Chinese Birth Month : Lunar Month 5
Chinese Birth Date : 19th
You are born between : 5-7pm
Your animal sign is : The Ox

THE SELF 1966-1975 6-15 — ● A3 Sun, △ A12 Scholar, B22 Completion — St4/Br10 *Rooster 5-7pm*

Color Code
Red   - Year under review
Blue   - The 10-Year Chart
Black - The Life Chart

The Catalysts
$ Prosperity
✿ Fame
♪ Power
■ Obstruction

Star Brightness
● Brilliant
o Bright
△ Twinkling
✕ Dark

TRAVEL 2026-2035 66-75 — St8/Br4 *Rabbit 5-7am*

ELDERS 1976-1985 16-25 — o A13 General, B23 Ram — St5/Br11 *Dog 7-9pm*

STAFF	2016-2025 56-65	CAREER	2006-2015 46-55	PROPERTIES	1996-2005 36-45	KARMIC	1986-1995 26-35
o A14 Pioneer B20 Delight B27 Void C29 The Lover		B18 Arts Minister ✿ B17 Literary Minister ■ C31 Opposition		o A1 Emperor B25 Fire		△ A2 Intelligence B21 Winged Horse	
St7/Br3 *Tiger 3-5am*		St8/Br2 *Ox 1-3am*		St7/Br1 *Rat 11pm-1am*		St6/Br12 *Pig 9-11pm*	

Career

A18 ARTS MINISTER (☼)   With the Arts Minister here and reflected by A10 Messenger($) in the opposite chamber, Diana acquired fame and fortune wherever she went. An ambassador for the unfortunate, she was able to draw in the crowd and was an admired envoy for the charities she presided over.

B17 LITERARY MINISTER (■)   With the Obstruction Catalyst in tow to the star of examinations and scholastic achievements, it was obvious why Diana never felt drawn to higher educational pursuits.

C31 OPPOSITION   An interesting combination of the star of decisiveness and endings, reflected by (A5) The Waif (building from nothing) and (B26) The Bell (a very difficult path). Indicative of her early eschewing of a short nondescript stint in teaching (The Arts and Literary Ministers), and carving out a place for herself in the eyes of royalty and ultimately, the world.

Staff

A14 THE PIONEER   She had independent-minded, even rebellious people under her.

B20 DELIGHT   This little star of guidance and protection unfortunately brought its own dosage of bitter-sweetness with exciting contacts with male staff members. Under the influence of the dark stars (see below), when all is said and done, it might have left more of a bitter after-taste.

C29 THE LOVER   This romantic star forms an enchanting pair with Happiness in the opposing chamber. However, surrounded by the dark stars (B27 Void, B24 Spinning Top, B28 Punishment), any solace Diana would have gotten from sympathetic staff members proved to be short-lived and in retrospect, back-fired.

Travel

Devoid of any star, those in the opposing house tell the story. (A12) The Scholar – who does not agree with traveling – brings problems when in a foreign land. (A3) The Sun (↗), with power attached reflecting the Travel Sector was to bring mega doses of fame wherever Diana went. However, this indicated more of a burn-out than being supportive of Diana. (B22) Completion: This lucky star brought material and spiritual wealth for Diana on her travels, as well as protection for her on the road. However, on that fateful night of 1997, Completion was too far away to exert any influence.

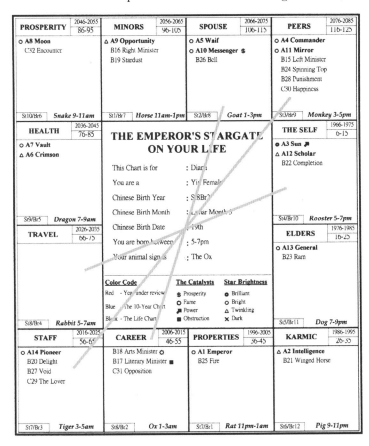

PROSPERITY	2046-2055 86-95	MINORS	2056-2065 96-105	SPOUSE	2066-2075 106-115	PEERS	2076-2085 116-125
○ A8 Moon C32 Encounter		△ A9 Opportunity B16 Right Minister B19 Stardust		○ A5 Waif ○ A10 Messenger $ B26 Bell		○ A4 Commander ○ A11 Mirror B15 Left Minister B24 Spinning Top B28 Punishment C30 Happiness	
St10/Br6	*Snake 9-11am*	St1/Br7	*Horse 11am-1pm*	St2/Br8	*Goat 1-3pm*	St3/Br9	*Monkey 3-5pm*

HEALTH	2036-2045 76-85				THE SELF	1966-1975 6-15
○ A7 Vault △ A6 Crimson					● A3 Sun ↗ △ A12 Scholar B22 Completion	

THE EMPEROR'S STARGATE ON YOUR LIFE

This Chart is for : Diana
You are a : Yin Female
Chinese Birth Year : St8Br2
Chinese Birth Month : Lunar Month 6
Chinese Birth Date : 19th
You are born between : 5-7pm
Your animal sign is : The Ox

St9/Br5	*Dragon 7-9am*				St4/Br10	*Rooster 5-7pm*

TRAVEL	2026-2035 66-75				ELDERS	1976-1985 16-25
					○ A13 General B23 Ram	

Color Code
Red - Year under review
Blue - The 10-Year Chart
Black - The Life Chart

The Catalysts
$ Prosperity
✿ Fame
↗ Power
■ Obstruction

Star Brightness
● Brilliant
○ Bright
△ Twinkling
✕ Dark

St8/Br4	*Rabbit 5-7am*				St5/Br11	*Dog 7-9pm*

STAFF	2016-2025 56-65	CAREER	2006-2015 46-55	PROPERTIES	1996-2005 36-45	KARMIC	1986-1995 26-35
○ A14 Pioneer B20 Delight B27 Void C29 The Lover		B18 Arts Minister ✿ B17 Literary Minister ■ C31 Opposition		○ A1 Emperor B25 Fire		△ A2 Intelligence B21 Winged Horse	
St7/Br3	*Tiger 3-5am*	St8/Br2	*Ox 1-3am*	St7/Br1	*Rat 11pm-1am*	St6/Br12	*Pig 9-11pm*

Health

A7 THE VAULT In the majority of books written about the late princess, Diana's health was not the most sought after of subjects discussed. However, from Stargate's perspective, the Vault in the Health sector has to do with the stomach, ribs or lungs. We can only point out, in retrospect that these were the areas that sustained the most serious injuries at her death.

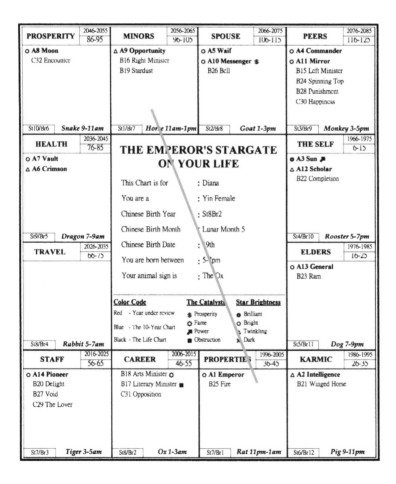

PROSPERITY	2046-2055 86-95	MINORS	2056-2065 96-105	SPOUSE	2066-2075 106-115	PEERS	2076-2085 116-125
o A8 Moon C32 Encounter		△ A9 Opportunity B16 Right Minister B19 Stardust		o A5 Waif o A10 Messenger $ B26 Bell		o A4 Commander o A11 Mirror B15 Left Minister B24 Spinning Top B28 Punishment C30 Happiness	
St10/Br6	Snake 9-11am	St1/Br7	Horse 11am-1pm	St2/Br8	Goat 1-3pm	St3/Br9	Monkey 3-5pm

HEALTH	2036-2045 76-85			THE SELF	1966-1975 6-15
o A7 Vault △ A6 Crimson		**THE EMPEROR'S STARGATE ON YOUR LIFE**		o A3 Sun ♫ o A12 Scholar B22 Completion	

This Chart is for : Diana
You are a : Yin Female
Chinese Birth Year : St8Br2
Chinese Birth Month : Lunar Month 5
Chinese Birth Date : 9th
You are born between : 5-7pm
Your animal sign is : The Ox

St9/Br5	Dragon 7-9am			St4/Br10	Rooster 5-7pm

TRAVEL	2026-2035 66-75			ELDERS	1976-1985 16-25
				o A13 General B23 Ram	

Color Code

Red - Year under review
Blue - The 10-Year Chart
Black - The Life Chart

The Catalysts

$ Prosperity
⊙ Fame
♫ Power
■ Obstruction

Star Brightness

● Brilliant
o Bright
☆ Twinkling
✕ Dark

St8/Br4	Rabbit 5-7am			St5/Br11	Dog 7-9pm

STAFF	2016-2025 56-65	CAREER	2006-2015 46-55	PROPERTIES	1996-2005 36-45	KARMIC	1986-1995 26-35
o A14 Pioneer B20 Delight B27 Void C29 The Lover		B18 Arts Minister ⊙ B17 Literary Minister ■ C31 Opposition		o A1 Emperor B25 Fire		△ A2 Intelligence B21 Winged Horse	
St7/Br3	Tiger 3-5am	St8/Br2	Ox 1-3am	St7/Br1	Rat 11pm-1am	St6/Br12	Pig 9-11pm

A6 CRIMSON   Pain or sicknesses relating to the blood. Psychological problems.

Prosperity

A8 THE MOON   The general source of wealth for Diana would have come from accumulated 'savings' or 'a nest egg'. These would point to lavish gifts and allowances she received in the capacity of the Princess of Wales; not to mention the priceless state jewelry that would have been at her disposal for life.

A32 ENCOUNTER   Because of the prosperity or the opulence that surrounded her, several clandestine liaisons were said to have developed. Manipulative and exploitative, none of the affairs blossomed and were cause for much chagrin (reflecting the Karmic Wealth house) for Diana.

Minors

A9 OPPORTUNITY   Sporty and elegant, many have been drawn to the princess.

B16 RIGHT MINISTER   The princes are honorable, kind and accepting and they also display a calm and elegant demeanor. However, without the support of the Left Minister at its opposing or 120° sectors, this star's other qualities – sexuality and seduction, may be causes for concern.

B19 STARDUST   This delightfully helpful star has found its way to the princes, ensuring an abundance of mentors and helpful people coming in throughout their lifetimes as and when necessary. Delight (B20), its counterpart at 120°, forms the pair and underscores the good fortune.

Opposing the Minors House

C25 FIRE   This dark star brings a catastrophe at an early age.

A1 EMPEROR   The Emperor reflects the Minors sector. This, together with the auspicious stars that surround, is an early indication of an ascension to the throne by one of the princes.

The Spouse

The Waif in The Spouse's chamber, indicated emotional turmoil, leading to unhappiness in the relationship.

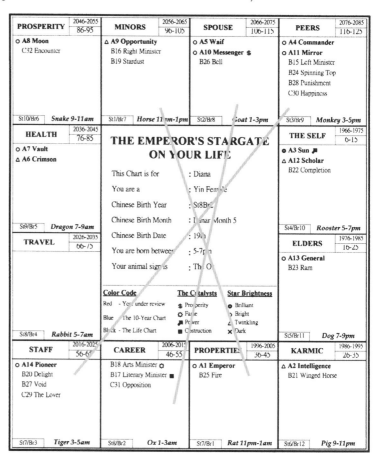

PROSPERITY	2046-2055 86-95	MINORS	2056-2065 96-105	SPOUSE	2066-2075 106-115	PEERS	2076-2085 116-125
o A8 Moon C32 Encounter		△ A9 Opportunity B16 Right Minister B19 Stardust		o A5 Waif o A10 Messenger $ B26 Bell		o A4 Commander o A11 Mirror B15 Left Minister B24 Spinning Top B28 Punishment C30 Happiness	
St10/Br6	Snake 9-11am	St1/Br7	Horse 11am-1pm	St2/Br8	Goat 1-3pm	St3/Br9	Monkey 3-5pm

THE EMPEROR'S STARGATE ON YOUR LIFE

This Chart is for : Diana
You are a : Yin Female
Chinese Birth Year : St8Br...
Chinese Birth Month : Lunar Month 5
Chinese Birth Date : 19th
You are born between : 5-7pm
Your animal sign is : The Ox

Color Code

Red - You under review
Blue - The 10-Year Chart
Black - The Life Chart

The Catalysts

$ Prosperity
✿ Fame
✈ Power
■ Construction

Star Brightness

● Brilliant
○ Bright
△ Twinkling
✕ Dark

HEALTH	2036-2045 76-85					THE SELF	1966-1975 6-15
o A7 Vault △ A6 Crimson						● A3 Sun ✈ △ A12 Scholar B22 Completion	
St9/Br5	Dragon 7-9am					St4/Br10	Rooster 5-7pm
TRAVEL	2026-2035 66-75					ELDERS	1976-1985 16-25
						o A13 General B23 Ram	
St8/Br4	Rabbit 5-7am					St5/Br11	Dog 7-9pm
STAFF	2016-2025 56-65	CAREER	2006-2015 46-55	PROPERTIES	1996-2005 36-45	KARMIC	1986-1995 26-35
o A14 Pioneer B20 Delight B27 Void C29 The Lover		B18 Arts Minister ✿ B17 Literary Minister ■ C31 Opposition		o A1 Emperor B25 Fire		△ A2 Intelligence B21 Winged Horse	
St7/Br3	Tiger 3-5am	St8/Br2	Ox 1-3am	St7/Br1	Rat 11pm-1am	St6/Br12	Pig 9-11pm

A10 THE MESSENGER $ Verbal (or non-verbal) disagreements with the loved one having to do with money; or – relationships with high profile, wealthy individuals.

B26 BELL A dark force, signifying rife and unpleasantness. Playing one against the other, these three dark stars in the marriage sector, unfortunately, reinforces the obvious. The fate of the marriage was sealed.

Peers

A4 COMMANDER	
A11 MIRROR	*Opposing the Peers House*
B15 THE LEFT MINISTER	**A14 THE PIONEER**
B24 THE SPINNING TOP	**B20 DELIGHT**
B28 PUNISHMENT	**B27 THE VOID**
C30 HAPPINESS	**C29 THE LOVER**

With a bright Commander (A4) and Mirror (A11), the Left Minister (B15) in the Peers sectors and a bright Pioneer (A14) opposing, it appeared that Diana's siblings and those she chose to be her allies, were strong, commanding people. However, with the Spinning Top (C24), Punishment (C28) and Void (C27) opposing – three of the five dark stars – in this sector, her enemies here equal in number to her sympathizers.

An interesting placement of Happiness reflected by the Lover (C29) in the Peers chamber. It was written in the stars that Diana should meet her future husband through one of her siblings.

CAREER	STAFF / PROSPERITY	STAFF	TRAVEL / MINORS	TRAVEL	HEALTH / SPOUSE	HEALTH	PROSPERITY / PEERS
o A8 Moon $ C32 Encounter		△ A9 Opportunity B16 Right Minister B19 Stardust		o A5 Waif ■ ⩘ o A10 Messenger $ ■ B26 Bell		o A4 Commander ⩘ o A11 Mirror B15 Left Minister B24 Spinning Top B28 Punishment C30 Happiness	
	Snake 9-11am		*Horse 11am-1pm*		*Goat 1-3pm*		*Monkey 3-5pm*

PROPERTIES	CAREER / HEALTH			PROSPERITY	MINORS / THE SELF
o A7 Vault ✪ △ A6 Crimson				o A3 Sun ⩘ $ △ A12 Scholar B22 Completion	

THE EMPEROR'S STARGATE
FOR AGE 37 (1997)

This Chart is for : Diana

You are a : Yin Female

Chinese Birth Year : St?Br2

Chinese Birth Month : Lunar Month 5

Chinese Birth Date : 19th

You are born between : 5-7pm

Your animal sign is : The Ox

Dragon 7-9am   *Rooster 5-7pm*

KARMIC	PROPERTIES / TRAVEL			MINORS	SPOUSE / ELDERS
				o A13 General B23 Ram	

Color Code   **The Catalysts**   **Star Brightness**

Red   - Year under review $ Prosperity   ● Brilliant

Blue   - The 10-Year Chart   ✪ Fame   o Bright

Black - The Life Chart   ⩘ Power   △ Twinkling

         ■ Obstruction   ✕ Dark

Rabbit 5-7am   *Dog 7-9pm*

ELDERS	KARMIC / STAFF	THE SELF	ELDERS / CAREER	PEERS	THE SELF / PROPERTIES	SPOUSE	PEERS / KARMIC
o A14 Pioneer B20 Delight B27 Void C29 The Lover		B18 Arts Minister ✪ B17 Literary Minister ■ C31 Opposition		o A1 Emperor B25 Fire		△ A2 Intelligence ✪ B21 Winged Horse	
	Tiger 3-5am		*Ox 1-3am*		*Rat 11pm-1am*		*Pig 9-11pm*

Diana's Stargate in 1997 – aged 37

With due respect to the late princess, we shall now look at Diana's chart in the year of her death. The Dark Stars were rife (altogether four in the Self and opposing) plus other indicators in the year of her death.

The Self

B17 LITERARY MINISTER (■)   Documentation that led to great losses – pointing to her divorce papers and separation agreements which finally came through.

A18 ARTS MINISTER (☼)   It was one of Diana's last wishes that she would like to continue to be a "Princess of the People". Still drawing in the crowds, this seemingly lucky star with fame attached, effectively became the catalyst of her demise. In Diana's case, Fame pursued relentlessly and eventually overtook her.

C31 OPPOSITION   Unfortunately, without any auspicious stars around and all the fearsome ones, this star was given full power to come to its own. It became the death knell.

Opposing the Minors House

The Travel sector

All three stars were dark and dangerous.

(A5) THE WAIF (■) (↗)   Power was with the Waif for Diana in the year 1997. The Waif had once again started from zero, with her innate ability to build from nothing and (more appropriate in Diana's case) to go from have, to not, and then to have again. However, the Waif's 10-year macabre dance with Obstruction still led. The Waif in retrograde invites disasters while in enjoyment. Diana was to have her heart broken – only this time, literally.

A10 THE MESSENGER ($)(■)   It was in Diana's Life Chart that she could move mountains using her voice. However, in the year 1997, the Messenger had taken on the Obstruction Catalyst. She had crossed the paparazzi ("messengers" in their own right) or they had crossed her. Here, without the protection (of the good stars) accorded her when she was "royal" and in a foreign land, this proved fatal.

B26 THE BELL   Without the benevolent rays of the Emperor (A1), Opportunity (A9), or The General (A13) nearby, Bell indicates "a lonesome individual and crippling injuries".

We shall also look at the houses pertaining to those who traveled with Diana on that fateful night.

The Spouse

A2 INTELLIGENCE (☼)   Fame begets Fame. As much as the paparazzi wouldn't stop pursuing Diana, they now had a new target, she and Dody, her companion.

B21 THE WINGED HORSE In the Spouse's sector, the husband can expect unswerving support from his wife, or the lady will be independently wealthy. However … if hemmed in by any dark star (here, we have B23 the Ram and B25 Fire in the sectors before and after), "the Winged Horse will encounter accidents or danger whilst on the road."

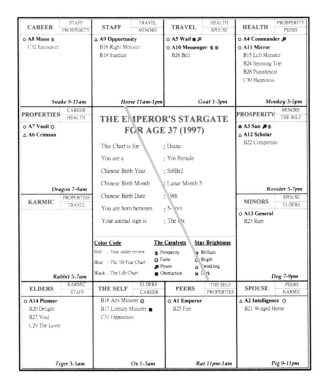

CAREER	STAFF / PROSPERITY	STAFF	TRAVEL / MINORS	TRAVEL	HEALTH / SPOUSE	HEALTH	PROSPERITY / PEERS
○ A8 Moon $ C32 Encounter		△ A9 Opportunity B16 Right Minister B19 Stardust		○ A5 Waif ■ ♪ ○ A10 Messenger $ ■ B26 Bell		○ A4 Commander ♪ ○ A11 Mirror B15 Left Minister B24 Spinning Top B28 Punishment C30 Happiness	
Snake 9-11am		*Horse 11am-1pm*		*Goat 1-3pm*		*Monkey 3-5pm*	

PROPERTIES	CAREER / HEALTH		PROSPERITY	MINORS / THE SELF
○ A7 Vault ○ △ A6 Crimson			○ A3 Sun ♪$ △ A12 Scholar B22 Completion	
Dragon 7-9am			*Rooster 5-7pm*	

THE EMPEROR'S STARGATE FOR AGE 37 (1997)

This Chart is for   : Diana
You are a   : Yin Female
Chinese Birth Year   : St8Br2
Chinese Birth Month   : Lunar Month 5
Chinese Birth Date   : 9th
You are born between : 5-?pm
Your animal sign is   : The Ox

Color Code	The Catalysts	Star Brightness
Red - Year under review	$ Prosperity	♪ Brilliant
Blue - The 10-Year Chart	○ Fame	C Bright
Black - The Life Chart	♪ Power	△ Twinkling
	■ Obstruction	x Dark

KARMIC	PROPERTIES / TRAVEL	MINORS	SPOUSE / ELDERS
		○ A13 General B23 Ram	
Rabbit 5-7am		*Dog 7-9pm*	

ELDERS	KARMIC / STAFF	THE SELF	ELDERS / CAREER	PEERS	THE SELF / PROPERTIES	SPOUSE	PEERS / KARMIC
○ A14 Pioneer B20 Delight B27 Void C29 The Lover		B18 Arts Minister ○ B17 Literary Minister ■ C31 Opposition		○ A1 Emperor B25 Fire		△ A2 Intelligence ○ B21 Winged Horse	
Tiger 3-5am		*Ox 1-3am*		*Rat 11pm-1am*		*Pig 9-11pm*	

Staff

(A9) Opportunity, **(B16) The Right Minister** *and* **(B19) Stardust** ruled this sector.

Opposing the Staff House:
(A1) The Emperor *and* **(B25) Fire**.

The lone dark star (Fire) left chaos and destruction in its wake. However, in the face of several bright, auspicious stars, its evil forces were kept just at bay. Sustaining serious injuries, Diana's bodyguard was the sole survivor in the car crash.

Nov. 14, 1948 10 PM

CAREER	ELDERS / STAFF	STAFF	KARMIC / TRAVEL	TRAVEL	PROPERTIES / HEALTH	HEALTH	CAREER / PROSPERITY
B22 Completion		△ A2 Intelligence ■ ♬ ○ B23 Ram C31 Opposition		△ A1 Emperor ✕ A14 Pioneer B20 Delight			
Snake 9-11am		*Horse 11am-1pm*		*Goat 1-3pm*		*Monkey 3-5pm*	

PROPERTIES	THE SELF / CAREER				PROSPERITY	STAFF / MINORS
△ A3 Sun ○ B24 Spinning Top		**THE EMPEROR'S STARGATE** **FOR AGE 50 (1997)**			○ A7 Vault B26 Bell C30 Happiness	
Dragon 7-9am					*Rooster 5-7pm*	

This Chart is for : Charles
You are a : Yang Male
Chinese Birth Year : St5Br1
Chinese Birth Month : Lunar Month 10
Chinese Birth Date : 14th
You are born between : 9–11pm
Your animal sign is : The Rat

KARMIC	PEERS / PROPERTIES				MINORS	TRAVEL / SPOUSE
△ A4 Commander ○ A13 General B18 Arts Minister C29 The Lover					△ A8 Moon ♬ $ B28 Punishment C32 Encounter	
Rabbit 5-7am					*Dog 7-9pm*	

Color Code
Red - Year under review
Blue - The 10-Year Chart
Black - The Life Chart

The Catalysts
$ Prosperity
○ Fame
♬ Power
■ Obstruction

Star Brightness
● Brilliant
○ Bright
△ Twinkling
✕ Dark

ELDERS	SPOUSE / KARMIC	THE SELF	MINORS / ELDERS	PEERS	PROSPERITY / THE SELF	SPOUSE	HEALTH / PEERS
○ A5 Waif $ ♬ ○ A12 Scholar B21 Winged Horse		△ A11 Mirror B15 Left Minister B16 Right Minister B19 Stardust B25 Fire		△ A10 Messenger ■ B27 Void		○ A6 Crimson ■ ○ A9 Opportunity $ B17 Literary Minister ○	
Tiger 3-5am		*Ox 1-3am*		*Rat 11pm-1am*		*Pig 9-11pm*	

160

Charles's chart in 1997

*I*n conclusion, it may be a point of interest to run Charles's chart for the same year, 1997. Diana's destiny would fall under the Peers sector, after the divorce.

Peers

(A10) The Messenger(■)
(B27) The Void

Opposing the Peers House
(A2) Intelligence(■)(↗)(✿)
(B23) The Ram
(C31) Finality

All these were dark, destroying stars. At 120°, an additional dark star (B24) The Spinning Top, presided. (A3) The Sun(✿), a lone bright star (with Fame attached which acted against Diana at any rate), proved too weak against six deadly ones.

Note: Diana's Birthdate - 1st July 1961 at 18:00 hours
*   Charles's Birthdate - 14th November 1948 at 22:00 hours*

10 A Sample Reading

Remember always that the universe is a friend and its ultimate intention is for you to attain success and harmony on all levels.

We're fascinated by reading tabloids and gossip items about the rich, famous, and infamous. Wouldn't it be grand to be able to read our own life in much the same way? Think of all the hoops and dead-ends that could have been avoided from the past and just to zoom in on the future to what's right for you, avoiding all the hang-cliffs altogether.

With Stargate now in hand, you will be able to do just that. Having come this far in the book, you will now have recognized there are very specific messages for you. Learn to recognize them and you are well on your way to success. Remember always that the universe is a friend and its ultimate intention is for you to attain success and harmony on all levels. There will be lessons to be learned, for sure. But you are not going against universal law by learning them in a few hours (with the help of Stargate). Nor will you be judged worthier by wallowing in disappointments and failures, banging your head against the wall for any length of time before coming around and attaining your goals. Think about that – the choice is yours!

To get further acquainted with the stars' messages, allow us to take your hand now and walk you through a reading we did for a client. Mr. Zhang, an entrepreneur, came to us earlier this year at the age of 44. Only major subjects of interest are highlighted e.g. The Life in general, career, relationships and in Mr. Zhang's case, a telling point about the children. Let's take a look …

SPOUSE 2063-2072 106-115	PEERS 2073-2082 116-125	THE SELF 1963-1972 6-15	ELDERS 1973-1982 16-25
△ **A1 Emperor** ○ **A13 General** B22 Completion B25 Fire C29 The Lover	B17 Literary Minister B23 Ram C31 Opposition	B20 Delight B26 Bell B27 Void	B18 Arts Mininster B21 Wing Horse
St4/Br6 *Snake 9-11am*	St5/Br7 *Horse 11am-1pm*	St6/Br8 *Goat 1-3pm*	St7/Br9 *Monkey 3-5pm*

MINORS 2053-2062 96-105		KARMIC 1983-1992 26-35
○ **A2 Intelligence** ■ ○ **A12 Scholar** B24 Spin Top		× **A6 Crimson** △ **A14 Pioneer**
St3/Br5 *Dragon 7-9am*		St8/Br10 *Rooster 5-7pm*

THE EMPEROR'S STARGATE
ON YOUR LIFE

This Chart is for : Mr. Zhang

You are a : Yang Male

Chinese Birth Year : St5Br11

Chinese Birth Month : Lunar Month 10

Chinese Birth Date : 24th

You are born between : 7-9am

Your animal sign is : The Dog

Color Code

Red - Year under review

Blue - The 10-Year Chart

Black - The Life Chart

The Catalysts

$ Prosperity

✿ Fame

♞ Power

■ Obstruction

Star Brightness

● Brilliant

○ Bright

△ Twinkling

× Dark

PROSPERITY 2043-2052 86-95		PROPERTIES 1993-2002 36-45
○ **A11 Mirror** B28 Punishmt		C32 Encounter
St2/Br4 *Rabbit 5-7am*		St9/Br11 *Dog 7-9pm*

HEALTH 2033-2042 76-85	TRAVEL 2023-2032 66-75	STAFF 2013-2022 56-65	CAREER 2003-2012 46-55
△ **A3 Sun** ♞ △ **A10 Messenger**	○ **A4 Commander** △ **A9 Opportunity** $ B15 Left Minister B16 Right Minister B19 Stardust	△ **A5 Waif** ○ **A8 Moon** ✿	● **A7 Vault** C30 Happiness
St1/Br3 *Tiger 3-5am*	St2/Br2 *Ox 1-3am*	St1/Br1 *Rat 11pm-1am*	St10/Br12 *Pig 9-11pm*

The Life

WHAT THE STARS SAY

We started with identifying the Auspicious stars. In Mr. Zhang's case, he has three pairs – (B15 and 16) The Left and Right Ministers in the same chamber and (B19 and 20) Stardust and Delight supporting each other at opposite chambers. Throughout the entire life, he will have friends and partners coming in at different times to help and support. Supporting the Self are (B17 and 18) The Literary and Arts Ministers.

The Dark Stars in the Self are (B26) Bell, indicating a lonesome childhood and its dark comrade in arms (B27) The Void, working against anything having to do with prosperity. This star, however, also stands for extraordinary ideas. With the input of hard work, this person can go where no one has been before.

THE LIFE IN CONCLUSION

Fortunately (A9) Opportunity with the Prosperity Catalyst in tow, indicates there are successes to be found on this travels or business trips. And the above three pairs of benevolent auspicious stars are more than enough ammunition to suppress the stinging rays of Bell and Void. This is not to say, though, there won't be several spells of difficulties and self-doubt in the life.

PROSPERITY	SPOUSE	MINORS	PEERS	SPOUSE	THE SELF	PEERS	ELDERS
△ A1 Emperor o A13 General B22 Completion B25 Fire C29 The Lover		B17 Literary Minister ■ B23 Ram C31 Opposition		B20 Delight B26 Bell B27 Void		B18 Arts Mininster ◢ B21 Wing Horse	
St4/Br6	*Snake 9-11am*	St5/Br7	*Horse 11am-1pm*	St6/Br8	*Goat 1-3pm*	St7/Br9	*Monkey 3-5pm*

HEALTH	MINORS		THE SELF	KARMIC
o A2 Intelligence ■ o A12 Scholar B24 Spin Top			× A6 Crimson △ A14 Pioneer	
St3/Br5	*Dragon 7-9am*		St8/Br10	*Rooster 5-7pm*

Stargate for the 10-year period 26-35 (1983-1992)

This Chart is for	: Mr. Zhang
You are a	: Yang Male
Chinese Birth Year	: St5Br11
Chinese Birth Month	: Lunar Month 10
Chinese Birth Date	: 24th
You are born between	: 7-9am
Your animal sign is	: The Dog

TRAVEL	PROSPERITY		ELDERS	PROPERTIES
o A11 Mirror B28 Punishmt			C32 Encounter	
St2/Br4	*Rabbit 5-7am*		St9/Br11	*Dog 7-9pm*

Color Code	The Catalysts	Star Brightness
Red - Year under review	$ Prosperity	● Brilliant
Blue - The 10-Year Chart	✿ Fame	o Bright
Black - The Life Chart	◢ Power	△ Twinkling
	■ Obstruction	× Dark

STAFF	HEALTH	CAREER	TRAVEL	PROPERTIES	STAFF	KARMIC	CAREER
△ A3 Sun ◢○ △ A10 Messenger $		o A4 Commander △ A9 Opportunity $ B15 Left Minister B16 Right Minister B19 Stardust		△ A5 Waif o A8 Moon ○		o A7 Vault C30 Happiness	
St1/Br3	*Tiger 3-5am*	St2/Br2	*Ox 1-3am*	St1/Br1	*Rat 11pm-1am*	St10/Br12	*Pig 9-11pm*

The Career

WHAT THE STARS SAY

With (A7) The Vault and (C30) Happiness in his career sector, opposed by other powerful and auspicious stars (A1) the Emperor, (A13) The General, (B22) Completion and (C29) The Lover, and only one detrimental star (B25) Fire, it was obvious Mr. Zhang could find success holding down a steady, lucrative career in a multi-national organization (which he did for a while).

This success can also be confirmed by his 10-year chart at age 26-35. All the successful stars were in his Career sector with only (B26) Bell and (B27) Void opposing. These were contained by (B19) Stardust and (B20) Delight.

THE CAREER IN CONCLUSION

During the years 26 to 35, Mr. Zhang's career took flight and it was obvious in retrospect that he had found his path to success. However, Mr. Zhang chose to start his own business during the next ten years. Let us take a look at how he fared.

HEALTH	SPOUSE	PROSPERITY	PEERS	MINORS	THE SELF	SPOUSE	ELDERS
△ **A1 Emperor** ○ ○ **A13 General** B22 Completion B25 Fire C29 The Lover		B17 Literary Minister B23 Ram C31 Opposition		B20 Delight B26 Bell B27 Void		B18 Arts Mininster B21 Wing Horse	
St4/Br6	**Snake 9-11am**	St5/Br7	**Horse 11am-1pm**	St6/Br8	**Goat 1-3pm**	St7/Br9	**Monkey 3-5pm**

TRAVEL	MINORS					PEERS	KARMIC
○ **A2 Intelligence** ■ ○ **A12 Scholar** $ B24 Spin Top						× **A6 Crimson** △ **A14 Pioneer**	

Stargate for the 10-year period
36-45 (1993-2002)

This Chart is for   : Mr. Zhang

You are a   : Yang Male

Chinese Birth Year   : St5Br11

Chinese Birth Month   : Lunar Month 10

Chinese Birth Date   : 24th

You are born between   : 7-9am

Your animal sign is   : The Dog

| St3/Br5 | **Dragon 7-9am** | | | | | St8/Br10 | **Rooster 5-7pm** |

STAFF	PROSPERITY					THE SELF	PROPERTIES
○ **A11 Mirror** B28 Punishmt						C32 Encounter	

Color Code   **The Catalysts**   **Star Brightness**

Red   - Year under review $ Prosperity   ● Brilliant

Blue   - The 10-Year Chart   ✿ Fame   ○ Bright

Black - The Life Chart   ➤ Power   △ Twinkling

                              ■ Obstruction   × Dark

| St2/Br4 | **Rabbit 5-7am** | | | | | St9/Br11 | **Dog 7-9pm** |

CAREER	HEALTH	PROPERTIES	TRAVEL	KARMIC	STAFF	ELDERS	CAREER
△ **A3 Sun** ➤ △ **A10 Messenger**		○ **A4 Commander** ■ △ **A9 Opportunity** $ B15 Left Minister B16 Right Minister B19 Stardust		△ **A5 Waif** ○ **A8 Moon** ○		● **A7 Vault** ➤ C30 Happiness	
St1/Br3	**Tiger 3-5am**	St2/Br2	**Ox 1-3am**	St1/Br1	**Rat 11pm-1am**	St10/Br12	**Pig 9-11pm**

The Business

WHAT THE STARS SAY

Mr. Zhang started his own business at age 36. During this current 10-year period (36-45), Mr. Zhang has one of his two Obstruction Catalysts in his Properties (business) sector. Obstruction attached to the Commander (A4), the star of earnings and rewards, in the Properties sector, should have been enough warning to deter Mr. Zhang from starting his venture at all *(refer to p. 121)*. But, how could he have known?

Moreover, the dark star (C32) Encounter resides in the Self and opposing are (B24) The Spinning Top and (A2) Intelligence, another obstructed star. It looked like the business was doomed to failure from the very start. Yes and no …

THE BUSINESS IN CONCLUSION

It is proving to be a long road ahead – a 10-year period of struggles, debts and near bankruptcy. The benevolent stars – (B15 and 16) The Left and Right Ministers, (B19 and 20) Stardust and Delight supporting each other at opposite chambers; (A12) The Scholar and (A9) Opportunity, both with Prosperity attached, all support. The business is still being kept afloat – for better or worse.

In retrospect, looking at the Career Sector with (A3) The Sun with Power attached, (A10) The Messenger and supported by (B18) The Arts Minister and (B21) The Winged Horse, Mr. Zhang would have chosen to stay in his Career – had he known. But he had begun the cycle and it is now in his karma to bring it to its conclusion as best he could.

TRAVEL	SPOUSE	HEALTH	PEERS	PROSPERITY	THE SELF	MINORS	ELDERS
△ A1 Emperor o A13 General B22 Completion B25 Fire C29 The Lover		B17 Literary Minister B23 Ram C31 Opposition		B20 Delight B26 Bell B27 Void		B18 Arts Mininster B21 Wing Horse	
St4/Br6	Snake 9-11am	St5/Br7	Horse 11am-1pm	St6/Br8	Goat 1-3pm	St7/Br9	Monkey 3-5pm

STAFF MINORS | **Stargate for the 10-year period** | **SPOUSE** KARMIC

STAFF	MINORS
o A2 Intelligence ■ o A12 Scholar B24 Spin Top	
St3/Br5 Dragon 7-9am	

Stargate for the 10-year period
46-55 (2003-2012)

This Chart is for	: Mr. Zhang
You are a	: Yang Male
Chinese Birth Year	: St5Br11
Chinese Birth Month	: Lunar Month 10
Chinese Birth Date	: 24th
You are born between	: 7-9am
Your animal sign is	: The Dog

SPOUSE	KARMIC
× A6 Crimson △ A14 Pioneer $	
St8/Br10 Rooster 5-7pm	

CAREER	PROSPERITY
o A11 Mirror B28 Punishmt	
St2/Br4 Rabbit 5-7am	

PEERS	PROPERTIES
C32 Encounter	
St9/Br11 Dog 7-9pm	

Color Code

Red	- Year under review
Blue	- The 10-Year Chart
Black	- The Life Chart

The Catalysts

$ Prosperity
☼ Fame
🎇 Power
■ Obstruction

Star Brightness

● Brilliant
o Bright
△ Twinkling
× Dark

PROPERTIES	HEALTH	KARMIC	TRAVEL	ELDERS	STAFF	THE SELF	CAREER
△ A3 Sun 🎇 △ A10 Messenger ☼		o A4 Commander △ A9 Opportunity $ ■ B15 Left Minister B16 Right Minister B19 Stardust		△ A5 Waif o A8 Moon ☼🎇		● A7 Vault C30 Happiness	
St1/Br3	Tiger 3-5am	St2/Br2	Ox 1-3am	St1/Br1	Rat 11pm-1am	St10/Br12	Pig 9-11pm

The next 10 years

CAREER OR BUSINESS?

Looking at Mr. Zhang's next 10-year chart (age 46-55), we see (A7) The Vault and (C30) Happiness in the Self, with The Emperor and General (A1 & A13) reflecting. Completion (B22) and (C29) The Lover completes this powerful, auspicious constellation. Fire (B25), although a dark star by nature, gets toned down with the General in the same house.

If Mr. Zhang were thinking of starting any new venture, this period would be the time. However, it is in his life lesson that an Obstruction catalyst, together with two dark stars, will always be reflecting his Properties (the business) house.

?
Ram in Peers
and Spin Top in Minors
P. 164 ?

On the other hand, the stars ruling the Career sector are powerful and positive. This is not to say Mr. Zhang would have to close his business and start looking for a job again! The service or consulting industry, or for that matter, any business venture that does not require Mr. Zhang investing his own money into it would be suitable.

The route to take is always made clear by Stargate. The choice, however, remains with us.

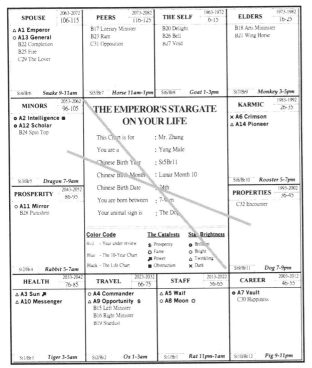

SPOUSE 2063-2072 106-115	PEERS 2073-2082 116-125	THE SELF 1963-1972 6-15	ELDERS 1973-1982 16-25
△ A1 Emperor ○ A13 General B22 Completion B25 Fire C29 The Lover	B17 Literary Minister B23 Ram C31 Opposition	B20 Delight B26 Bell B27 Void	B18 Arts Minister B21 Wing Horse
St4/Br6 *Snake 9-11am*	St5/Br7 *Horse 11am-1pm*	St6/Br8 *Goat 1-3pm*	St7/Br9 *Monkey 3-5pm*

MINORS 2053-2062 96-105		KARMIC 1983-1992 26-35
○ A2 Intelligence ■ ○ A12 Scholar B24 Spin Top		× A6 Crimson △ A14 Pioneer

THE EMPEROR'S STARGATE ON YOUR LIFE

This Chart is for	: Mr. Zhang
You are a	: Yang Male
Chinese Birth Year	: St5Br11
Chinese Birth Month	: Lunar Month 10
Chinese Birth Date	: 24th
You are born between	: 7-9 pm
Your animal sign is	: The Dog

Color Code		The Catalysts		Sta. Brightness	
Red	- Year under review	$ Prosperity		○ Brilliant	
Blue	- The 10-Year Chart	○ Fame		○ Bright	
Black	- The Life Chart	✿ Power		△ Twinkling	
		■ Obstruction		× Dark	

St3/Br5 *Dragon 7-9am*	St8/Br10 *Rooster 5-7pm*
PROSPERITY 2043-2052 86-95	PROPERTIES 1993-2002 36-45
○ A11 Mirror B28 Punishmt	C32 Encounter

St2/Br4 *Rabbit 5-7am*	St9/Br11 *Dog 7-9pm*

HEALTH 2033-2042 76-85	TRAVEL 2023-2032 66-75	STAFF 2013-2022 56-65	CAREER 2003-2012 46-55
△ A3 Sun ✿ △ A10 Messenger	○ A4 Commander ○ A9 Opportunity $ B15 Left Minister B16 Right Minister B19 Stardust	△ A5 Waif ○ A8 Moon ○	○ A7 Vault C30 Happiness
St1/Br3 *Tiger 3-5am*	St2/Br2 *Ox 1-3am*	St1/Br1 *Rat 11pm-1am*	St10/Br12 *Pig 9-11pm*

TRAVEL	HEALTH / SPOUSE	HEALTH	PROSPERITY / PEERS	PROSPERITY	MINORS / THE SELF	MINORS	SPOUSE / ELDERS
△ A1 Emperor ☆⚑ o A13 General B22 Completion B25 Fire C29 The Lover		B17 Literary Minister B23 Ram C31 Opposition		B20 Delight B26 Bell B27 Void		B18 Arts Mininster B21 Wing Horse	
St4/Br6 Snake 9-11am		St5/Br7 Horse 11am-1pm		St6/Br8 Goat 1-3pm		St7/Br9 Monkey 3-5pm	

THE EMPEROR'S STARGATE
FOR AGE 38 (1995)

STAFF	TRAVEL / MINORS		SPOUSE	PEERS / KARMIC
o A2 Intelligence ■ $ o A12 Scholar $☼ B24 Spin Top			× A6 Crimson △ A14 Pioneer	
St3/Br5 Dragon 7-9am			St8/Br10 Rooster 5-7pm	

This Chart is for : Mr. Zhang

You are a : Yang Male

Chinese Birth Year : St5Br11

Chinese Birth Month : Lunar Month 10

Chinese Birth Date : 24th

You are born between : 7-9am

Your animal sign is : The Dog

CAREER	STAFF / PROSPERITY		PEERS	THE SELF / PROPERTIES
o A11 Mirror B28 Punishmt			C32 Encounter	
St2/Br4 Rabbit 5-7pm			St9/Br11 Dog 7-9pm	

Color Code

Red - Year under review

Blue - The 10-Year Chart

Black - The Life Chart

The Catalysts
- $ Prosperity
- ☼ Fame
- ⚑ Power
- ■ Obstruction

Star Brightness
- ⊙ Brilliant
- o Bright
- △ Twinkling
- × Dark

PROPERTIES	CAREER / HEALTH	KARMIC	PROPERTIES / TRAVEL	ELDERS	KARMIC / STAFF	THE SELF	ELDERS / CAREER
△ A3 Sun ⚑ △ A10 Messenger		o A4 Commander ■ △ A9 Opportunity $ B15 Left Minister B16 Right Minister B19 Stardust		△ A5 Waif o A8 Moon ☼■		o A7 Vault ⚑ C30 Happiness	
St1/Br3 Tiger 3-5am		St2/Br2 Ox 1-3am		St1/Br1 Rat 11pm-1am		St10/Br12 Pig 9-11pm	

The Relationships

WHAT THE STARS SAY

At age 26-35, Mr. Zhang was looking to finding the right girl, fall in love and settle down. However, that was not to be. It is an intricate Stargate rule that when it comes to relationships, the 'bad' stars are what they are – (B26) Bell and (B27) Void in the *P. 166* Spouse's Chamber. However, the normally considered 'good' ones – (B20) Delight in the Spouse and (opposing) (B19) Stardust, The Commander, Opportunity, and the Left and Right Ministers,

in the context of a relationship, are just sparks in the air – illusions, flirtations or affairs destined to fizzle out.

The Lover-Happiness were in Spouse-Career houses at birth!

THE RELATIONSHIP IN CONCLUSION

It was not to be until 1995 that Mr. Zhang met and married the woman of his dreams. That year, (C30) Happiness and *in Spouse* (C29) The Lover faced each *house at birth,* other in the Self Sector. *← Also happened in 1983* Looking back at his Life Chart – these stars fall right over his *P. 164* Spouse and Career sectors. It was pre-destined he would *The 10-year chart did* marry someone he knew *not point* through work, a colleague. *to this event, but did not prevent it either.*

PROSPERITY	SPOUSE	MINORS	PEERS	SPOUSE	THE SELF	PEERS	ELDERS
△ A1 Emperor ○ A13 General B22 Completion B25 Fire C29 The Lover		B17 Literary Minister ■ B23 Ram C31 Opposition		B20 Delight B26 Bell B27 Void		B18 Arts Mininster ♫ B21 Wing Horse	
St4/Br6	Snake 9-11am	St5/Br7	Horse 11am-1pm	St6/Br8	Goat 1-3pm	St7/Br9	Monkey 3-5pm
HEALTH	MINORS					THE SELF	KARMIC
○ A2 Intelligence ■ ○ A12 Scholar B24 Spin Top						× A6 Crimson △ A14 Pioneer	
St3/Br5	Dragon 7-9am					St8/Br10	Rooster 5-7pm
TRAVEL	PROSPERITY					ELDERS	PROPERTIES
○ A11 Mirror B28 Punishmt						C32 Encounter	
St2/Br4	Rabbit 5-7am					St9/Br11	Dog 7-9pm
STAFF	HEALTH	CAREER	TRAVEL	PROPERTIES	STAFF	KARMIC	CAREER
△ A3 Sun ♫○ △ A10 Messenger $		○ A4 Commander △ A9 Opportunity $ B15 Left Minister B16 Right Minister B19 Stardust		△ A5 Waif ○ A8 Moon ○		● A7 Vault C30 Happiness	
St1/Br3	Tiger 3-5am	St2/Br2	Ox 1-3am	St1/Br1	Rat 11pm-1am	St10/Br12	Pig 9-11pm

Stargate for the 10-year period 26-35 (1983-1992)

This Chart is for : Mr. Zhang
You are a : Yang Male
Chinese Birth Year : St6Br11
Chinese Birth Month : Lunar Month 10
Chinese Birth Date : 24th
You are born between : 7-9am
Your animal sign is : The Dog

Color Code
Red - Year under review
Blue - The 10-Year Chart
Black - The Life Chart

The Catalysts
$ Prosperity
☼ Fame
♫ Power
■ Obstruction

Star Brightness
● Brilliant
○ Bright
△ Twinkling
× Dark

The Children

WHAT THE STARS SAY

It is the Stargate practitioner's training to be extra sensitive to the Obstruction Catalyst and where it should be resting at any particular period. When alerted to its place in the Minors Sectors during the 10-year period from age 26-35, Mr. Zhang offered an explanation: In a couple of close, albeit ended relationships, there have been a number of terminated pregnancies.

THE CHILDREN IN CONCLUSION

Mr. Zhang's Life Chart tells the same story – with the Obstruction Catalyst attached to (A2) Intelligence – the children's lives were at risk. There's also (B24) The Spinning Top, another dark star which lends strength to an already bleak situation. (A12) The Scholar, also in this house, tells of the late arrival of children. Mr. Zhang now has two boys, both being born after he turned 40.

SPOUSE 2063-2072 106-115	PEERS 2073-2082 116-125	THE SELF 1963-1972 6-15	ELDERS 1973-1982 16-25
△ A1 Emperor ○ A13 General B22 Completion B25 Fire C29 The Lover	B17 Literary Minister B23 Ram C31 Opposition	B20 Delight B26 Bell B27 Void	B18 Arts Mininster B21 Wing Horse
St4/Br6 *Snake 9-11am*	St5/Br7 *Horse 11am-1pm*	St6/Br8 *Goat 1-3pm*	St7/Br9 *Monkey 3-5pm*

MINORS 2053-2062 96-105		KARMIC 1983-1992 26-35
○ A2 Intelligence ■ ○ A12 Scholar B24 Spin Top	**THE EMPEROR'S STARGATE ON YOUR LIFE** This Chart is for : Mr. Zhang You are a : Yang Male Chinese Birth Year : St5Br11 Chinese Birth Month : Lunar Month 10 Chinese Birth Date : 24th You are born between : 7-9am Your animal sign is : The Dog	× A6 Crimson △ A14 Pioneer
St3/Br5 *Dragon 7-9am*		St8/Br10 *Rooster 5-7pm*

PROSPERITY 2043-2052 86-95	Color Code / The Catalysts / Star Brightness	PROPERTIES 1993-2002 36-45
○ A11 Mirror B28 Punishmt	**Color Code**	**The Catalysts**	**Star Brightness**
	Red - Year under review	$ Prosperity	○ Brilliant	C32 Encounter
	Blue - The 10-Year Chart	○ Fame	○ Bright	
	Black - The Life Chart	◢ Power	△ Twinkling	
		■ Obstruction	× Dark	
St2/Br4 *Rabbit 5-7am*		St9/Br11 *Dog 7-9pm*

HEALTH 2033-2042 76-85	TRAVEL 2023-2032 66-75	STAFF 2013-2022 56-65	CAREER 2003-2012 46-55
△ A3 Sun ◢ △ A10 Messenger	○ A4 Commander △ A9 Opportunity $ B15 Left Minister B16 Right Minister B19 Stardust	△ A5 Waif ○ A8 Moon ○	○ A7 Vault C30 Happiness
St1/Br3 *Tiger 3-5am*	St2/Br2 *Ox 1-3am*	St1/Br1 *Rat 11pm-1am*	St10/Br12 *Pig 9-11pm*